SAN

TAPE

BY
MICHAEL
GRANT

CORPORATE
PROFILES BY
CHARLES W. ROSS

TOWERY PUBLISHING, INC.

DIEGO

STORY

ART
DIRECTOR
BRIAN GROPPE

PHOTO
EDITOR
JERRY RIFE

MEMPHIS TENNESSEE, 1992

LIBRARY OF CONGRESS CATALOGING-IN-PUBLICATION DATA
Grant, Michael, 1943-
    San Diego tapestry / Michael Grant : corporate profiles by Charles
W. Ross.
       p. cm. — (Urban tapestry series)
    Includes index.
    ISBN 0-9628128-3-8 : $39.50
    1. San Diego (Calif.)—Pictorial works.   2. San Diego (Calif.)—
Description and travel.   3. San Diego (Calif.)—Industries.
I. Ross, Charles W. (Charles William), 1927- .   II. Title.
III. Series.
F869.S22G717 1992
979.4'985—dc20
                        91-65841
                        CIP

TOWERY Publishing, Inc.
1835 Union Avenue, Suite 142
Memphis, Tennessee 38104

PUBLISHER: J. Robert Towery
EXECUTIVE PUBLISHER: Meredith W. Grant
EDITOR: Patricia M. Towery
MANAGING EDITOR: Michael James
ASSISTANT ART DIRECTOR: Anne Castrodale
EDITORIAL CONSULTANT: Roger M. Showley

Printed in the United States of America

**URBAN
TAPESTRY
SERIES**

CONTENTS

PATTERNS
FROM
THE PAST

HISTORIANS DON'T GIVE JUAN RODRIGUEZ CABRILLO MUCH SPACE IN THEIR TEXTS ABOUT THE GREAT EXPLORERS. CABRILLO, THEY SAY, SIMPLY CAME ALONG WITH MANY OTHER SAILOR-ENTREPRENEURS IN THE WAKE OF CHRISTOPHER COLUMBUS, WHO WITH HIS EPIC 1492 VOYAGE PROVED THAT DISCOVERING NEW WORLDS COULD BE HISTORIC AND PROFITABLE. ♦ MOST SAN DIEGANS, HOWEVER, KNOW WHO CABRILLO WAS. A HANDSOME SANDSTONE STATUE OF HIM STANDS HIGH ON THE PROMONTORY AT POINT LOMA OVERLOOKING THE MOUTH OF THE BAY INTO WHICH HE SAILED WITH TWO SHIPS AND ABOUT 200 MEN ON SEPTEMBER 28, 1542. HE CLAIMED THE PLACE FOR SPAIN, OVER WHATEVER OBJECTIONS THE RESIDENT DIEGUEÑO INDIANS MIGHT HAVE RAISED, AND HE NAMED THE PLACE "SAN MIGUEL." ♦ TODAY, SPREAD AT CABRILLO'S FEET, IS A SPRAWLING, SUNNY CITY THAT, LIKE ITS DISCOVERER, HISTORICALLY HAS BEEN UNDER-RECOGNIZED. IT HAS BEEN A SAN DIEGO TRADITION TO LIKE IT THAT WAY, THOUGH EVEN TRADITIONALISTS NOW ADMIT THAT IT IS DIFFICULT TO KEEP THE NATION'S SIXTH LARGEST CITY UNDER WRAPS. ♦ OF COURSE, CABRILLO DID NOT "DISCOVER" SAN DIEGO, BUT HE WAS THE FIRST EUROPEAN TO SET FOOT ON THE PROMONTORY AT 32 DEGREES, 43 MINUTES N., 117 DEGREES, 10 MINUTES W., A LOCATION WHICH WOULD BE THE MOST POWERFUL INFLUENCE ON THE PERSONALITY OF THE CITY THAT GREW THERE. ♦ CABRILLO FOUND A NATURAL HARBOR WITH A SOUTH-FACING ENTRY BETWEEN POINT LOMA AND NORTH ISLAND THAT CARRIED NORTH AND CURVED AROUND NORTH ISLAND IN AN INVERTED U, THEN PROCEEDED SOUTH BETWEEN THE MAINLAND AND A LONG, WIDE SAND SPIT THAT CONNECTED NORTH ISLAND WITH THE MAINLAND SOME MILES TO THE SOUTH. THE OCEAN WATER WAS COLD, FED BY A STRONG CURRENT COMING DOWN THE COASTLINE FROM THE NORTH. ♦ BEYOND A NARROW COASTAL PLAIN, TO THE SOUTH AND EAST, WERE LOW RUGGED MOUNTAINS. DOWN FROM THE EAST MOUNTAINS CAME AN ENERGETIC RIVER THROUGH A VALLEY NORTH OF THE HARBOR. THE RIVER HAD

From her romantic beginnings until today—under the dramatic skies of the present—San Diego has taken dead aim on the brightest of 21st-century futures.
(Jerry Rife photo)

over the millennia laid down a wide delta that filled in the coastal plain from the harbor north to another bay that, in time, came to be called False Bay. The river's energy and the delta's circumstances were such that, at times, the river might empty into the harbor and, at other times, into False Bay.

Beyond the river valley, a broad mesa fed northward to more mountains. The narrow coastal flatland gave land access northwest to whatever discoveries lay there.

Indians, some of them, gave Cabrillo tentative greeting. They were the distant descendants of people who had crossed a prehistoric land bridge from Asia and spread out across the continent. These Indians eyeing Cabrillo were called the Diegueños. They were numerous in the area and, at that time of year, were living in the open and not wearing much.

The weather was delightful—like the Mediterranean, only nicer. The cold current from the north deflected most of the tropical closeness wanting to rise up from the south, and the Pacific hurricanes, or *chubascos*, rarely got through. Many sailors who followed Cabrillo's course here through the centuries would say it was the best climate on earth, with mild winters and a long summer that extended into October. Artists invariably interpret Cabrillo arriving at San Diego under dramatic skies, and historians think the region was wetter then than it is now. But on September 28, even 450 years later, a San Diegan would be apt to argue that Cabrillo must have arrived under hot, cloudless skies.

The conditions were both inviting and restricting. It was inevitable in human history that people would be attracted to the sun, the sea, and the topography that keynote this part of the world. But the east and south mountains hugged this population to the shoreline, and farther east beyond the mountains were true deserts.

The prevailing breeze off the ocean cooled the coastal plain, and, after a time, the Spanish explorers (the first in this region) noticed something unusual. The Indians had developed the practice of setting fires in order to herd game into central killing grounds. The smoke from these fires rose to a certain altitude and then collected, as if trapped against a ceiling. This was because the sea, as it had always done in this place, was driving a wedge of cool air onshore. Over land, the warm air rose, as warm air always does. But the layer of warm air over the layer of cold created an inversion, which interrupted the normal circulation of air away from the earth's surface.

The inversion hovered above the coastal plain, contained there between the eastern mountains and the onshore breeze. Into this "basin" poured smoke from the Indians' fires and from the fires of all the rest of the people to come. Then came the sun, to cook this particulate stew and set off photochemical reactions. They wouldn't call it "smog" for another 400-odd years after Cabrillo's arrival, but the irony was already evident. The same three elements—sun, sea, and topography—that attracted people to the area collaborated to drape a visible reminder over their golden land that Paradise would have its limits.

A second Spanish explorer, Sebastián Vizcaíno, visited at San Miguel in 1602 and renamed it San Diego de Alcalá after a Franciscan

> MANY SAILORS WHO FOLLOWED CABRILLO'S COURSE HERE THROUGH THE CENTURIES WOULD SAY IT WAS THE BEST CLIMATE ON EARTH, WITH MILD WINTERS AND A LONG SUMMER THAT EXTENDED INTO OCTOBER.

saint, St. Didacus of Alcalá. After Vizcaíno's visit, there is no record of any European activity in the San Diego area for more than 150 years, until the arrival of Father Junípero Serra in 1769. Father Serra established a series of missions in California, the first on July 16, 1769 in San Diego on Presidio Hill overlooking the two bays. Beginning with Father Serra, the stamp of Spanish civilization and *rancho* architecture would forever remain on California.

The patterns of settlement that would distinguish San Diego from Los Angeles started to show up with the expeditions of Don Juan Bautista de Anza. Commissioned by Spain to find a land route from Mexico into California, Anza broke a trail from the Colorado River in 1774 to 1776 that crossed the desert more or less parallel with the present Mexican border. It was then deflected north by the high mountains to a pass called San Carlos. The pass, at the northwestern corner of the Borrego Valley, pointed Anza and his settlers and missionaries through the coastal range to Father Serra's San Gabriel Mission in the wide basin that would become Los Angeles. That was the basic route followed for the next 150 years by settlers and commerce arriving from the south and east.

Commerce-hungry San Diegans in the late 1800s saw salvation in the promise of a southern transcontinental railroad with its western terminus at San Diego. With the mountains blocking the way, two possible routes were considered, but one was too far north, at San Gorgonio, and the other too far south.

With California's admission to the Union in 1850, the international boundary became, for San Diego, another physical boundary. The proposed southern railroad route, praised by surveyors as maybe the best in California, unfortunately crossed the Mexican border in its progress east and through the mountains down to the desert.

Eventually, the big line, the Southern Pacific, chose the wide San Gorgonio pass to Los Angeles. San Francisco and Los Angeles, with established links to the east by the late 1800s, began their transformations into major business centers. Los Angeles sought development of a deep-water port, after some haggling over Santa Monica or San Pedro as the better location. During that debate, one engineer said that if the city fathers wanted a good harbor, they should "move Los Angeles to San Diego."

SAN DIEGO DID WHAT ANY SUNNY COASTAL CITY WOULD DO THAT WAS CUT OFF ON ONE SIDE BY MOUNTAINS AND BORDERED ON THE OTHER BY THE SEA. IT DEVELOPED INTO ONE OF THE PRETTIEST CITIES IN THE WORLD, AND INTO THAT REPUTATION WAS BUILT A "SLEEPY VILLAGE" MYSTIQUE.

San Diego, meanwhile, did what any sunny coastal city would do that was cut off on one side by mountains and bordered on the other by the sea. It developed into one of the prettiest cities in the world, and into that reputation was built a "sleepy village" mystique. San Diego, with her Spanish heritage and easy pace, became more associated with Latin latitudes and attitudes than with the bustle of a nation driven by the expanding pressures of the industrial engine.

From the census of 1890 to the census of 1900, the population of San Diego County grew from 34,987 to 35,090. "It was," wrote San Diego historian Richard F. Pourade, "as if nobody had arrived or left, or had been born or died." Los Angeles, meanwhile, had a city population of more than 100,000, and in the county, 170,300. Commercially, San Diego might have possessed the uncertain geography, in the national mind-set, of a branch-office town at the end of a Santa Fe spur. To this day, San Diegans have to put up with such Eastern media affronts as calling La Jolla "a coastal jewel near Los Angeles."

Aesthetically, though, San Diego sat in her own private spotlight. Climate, some city leaders recognized, was a commodity to be promoted across the country to frozen Easterners. That realization touched off a local "smokestacks or geraniums" debate between the aesthetic and industrial camps that would go on for decades. There was no doubt that San Diego grew some sweet geraniums. By the turn of the century, the branch-office town was already becoming the mailing address for company presidents. Illinois publisher Edward Wyllis Scripps, from the age of 36, ran his newspaper empire from his sprawling ranch, Miramar, on the wide mesa north of downtown San Diego. And while Los Angeles had its charms and all the movie stars lived there, San Diegans remember glimpsing those celebrities in their big Packards and boat-tail Duesenbergs rumbling down the Torrey Pines Grade on U.S. 101, headed for the cosmopolitan pursuits in San Diego and Tijuana. Douglas Fairbanks had a ranch near the foot of the grade. Bing Crosby in the 1930s was the principal figure in the construction of a racetrack at Del Mar.

Even as the city developed its personality, events were under way that would provide San Diego an economic base for the 20th century. That base, in turn, would evolve into a technological compass that would point the city toward the 21st century. These were huge economic forces related to world conflict, and they would reach San Diego, not by the land routes so eagerly sought, but, as she had been discovered once before, from the sea.

COMMERCE-HUNGRY SAN DIEGANS IN THE LATE 1800s SAW SALVATION IN THE PROMISE OF A SOUTHERN TRANSCONTINENTAL RAILROAD WITH ITS WESTERN TERMINUS AT SAN DIEGO.

At the end of the 19th century, San Diegans started to feel the influence of events in Washington and the newspaper wars raging in New York City. Those were the days of sensationalism in the press, when legitimate daily newspapers had much the same flavor as today's supermarket tabloids. Sensationalism had been used to sell newspapers in the United States since 1830, but the technique was refined to an art by Joseph Pulitzer at *The New York World* around 1895, and bastardized into the lamentable "yellow press" by William Randolph Hearst at the rival *New York Journal*.

A popular notion in the nation at that time was "manifest destiny," and one of the main media topics was Cuban insurrection against Spain. Since the 1840s, manifest destiny had fueled the American belief that the country was compelled (by God Himself, some argued) to expand westward, to and beyond its Pacific shore, and to manage peace across the width and breadth of the hemisphere. It was a mandate that gave Americans every right, so they believed, to intervene in Cuban affairs.

If any Americans missed that point, the New York newspapers, Hearst's in particular, made sure they were brought up to speed. After 1895, circumstances of the Cuban revolt were carefully chronicled and occasionally frosted with some fiction, with the intent of spurring the nation toward the fulfillment of its "destiny" while selling a few newspapers at the same time. This was the time of the supposed exchange between Hearst and the artist Frederic Remington, whom Hearst had sent (as part of a large staff) to Havana in preparation for war. Weeks dragged by with no action, and Remington cabled Hearst that he was returning home. Supposedly Hearst cabled back: "Please remain. You furnish the pictures, and I'll furnish the war."

The cable story may be apocryphal, but more than one historian eventually would call it "Hearst's war." It lasted four months and inspired the United States' annexation of another Spanish colony, the Philippines. U.S. naval forces, expanding into Pacific waters after 1895, took note of the harbor that Sebastián Vizcaíno in 1602 described as "the best to be found in all the South Sea." Vizcaíno, ironically, was one of the Spanish adventurers who piloted the first "Manila galleons" from New Spain (Mexico) across the Pacific to the Philippines, bringing about the Spanish colonization there.

With Spanish-American tensions rising, the War Department in 1896 spent $1.5 million to emplace cannon batteries at Ballast Point and on Point Loma and North Island, in the event of any modern-day Spanish incursions into the harbor. Then, on George Washington's birthday in 1897, this new relationship between city and military bloomed into a full-blown love affair. San Diego planned to celebrate the holiday in

AT THE END OF THE 19TH CENTURY, SAN DIEGANS STARTED TO FEEL THE INFLUENCE OF EVENTS IN WASHINGTON AND THE NEWSPAPER WARS RAGING IN NEW YORK CITY.

grand style, with concerts, a sham battle, and parades on land and water. City fathers invited the Navy to join in, and the Navy accepted. Historian Pourade reported that most of the Pacific fleet, 10,000 tourists, and John Philip Sousa's band arrived in town for the event.

Now, harbor parades are one of San Diego's oldest and prettiest traditions, particularly the parade at Christmastime—the vessels all strung with lights, and carolers' voices floating across the water. But organizers of the modern parades may weep with envy on reading Pourade's account of the Washington's birthday parade, February 22, 1897:

"At 7:30 o'clock that night there was not a light to be seen on the water or along the shore. Then at a signal from the *U.S.S. Philadelphia's* salute gun, every electric light in the fleet was turned on and hundreds of colored torches were lighted. Aboard the *H.M.S. Camus* lighted Japanese lanterns were passed from hand to hand to the top of her rigging. As they reached the mastheads a bugle sounded and the *Camus* fired a barrage of colored rockets. Other men-of-war followed suit. The crowds on the beach gasped in wonder as the thousands of electric lights against a black velvet sky revealed the fleet anchored close in, bow on stern. More than fifty small boats rowed by Navy seamen led a procession of yachts and civilian craft lighted by electric lights and 6,000 colored torches. Then with fireworks rocketing overhead and star shells bursting, a band and a hundred-voice chorus on barges rendered *The Star-Spangled Banner...*"

The Spanish threat passed quickly, though obviously American interests in the Pacific did not. While the Great War was being fought in Europe, Japan interpreted the Philippines annexation as American imperialism and stepped up its own empire-building. America became watchful. Navy development around San Diego Harbor continued and by the early 1930s had killed two birds with one stone: dredging of the harbor provided the fill on which Lindbergh Field was built and created a turning basin for the Navy's biggest ships. In 1931, the *Saratoga* became the first of the giant new aircraft carriers to enter the harbor. That event also signaled the Navy's intention to establish its principal Pacific Coast air facility here.

San Diego's association with the romance of flying had already been established by an intrepid young pilot and an airplane that was built in 60 days in the spring of 1927 by Ryan Airlines of San Diego. In the 1920s, aviation reached a point where a trans-Atlantic flight became conceivable. A $25,000 prize was offered for the first pilot who could fly an airplane non-stop from New York to Paris.

Charles A. Lindbergh, 25, a mail pilot from St. Louis, got the fever, but he needed a suitable craft. In magazine advertisements he learned of a wing-over monoplane being produced in San Diego by the Ryan company. Lindbergh came to San Diego and on February 28, 1927, signed a contract for a modified version of Ryan's M-2 monoplane. It was built in Ryan's facilities on the waterfront and on Dutch Flats, north of Barnett Avenue. The plane was not quite 28 feet long and cost $10,580. Its registration number was N-X-211, but Lindbergh named the plane the

Spirit of St. Louis, in honor of his backers from St. Louis.

On April 28, Lindbergh took the plane on its first test flight. On May 10, he took off from North Island and flew east over the Cuyamaca Mountains toward New York. On May 12, he reached New York, and, on May 20, the *Spirit of St. Louis* took off for Paris. Late the next evening Ryan's little monoplane touched down in history at Le Bourget Field, Paris. The feat is commemorated on a plaque in the East Terminal at San Diego's busy Lindbergh Field.

East of the Lindbergh Field runways, paralleling Interstate 5 for a good mile, sits a long string of white assembly plant buildings. The first of these, dedicated in 1935, marked the relocation of the Consolidated Aircraft Corporation from Buffalo, New York, to San Diego. Again, it was the harbor, indirectly this time, that brought new life to the city. The company had a Navy contract to build PBY and PB2Y seaplanes, and, for half the year, water tests were difficult on the frozen reaches of northern New York. Consolidated needed a warm-weather site, preferably with an air terminal and a sheltered harbor nearby. San Diego filled that bill exactly.

In World War II, Consolidated (later Consolidated Vultee, or "Convair") built thousands of B-24 Liberator heavy bombers in those buildings, the foundation of an aerospace industry that would grow and thrive in San Diego, becoming the cornerstone of the city's modern industrial base.

U.S. NAVAL FORCES, EXPANDING INTO PACIFIC WATERS AFTER 1895, TOOK NOTE OF THE HARBOR THAT SEBASTIAN VIZCAINO IN 1602 DESCRIBED AS "THE BEST TO BE FOUND IN ALL THE SOUTH SEA."

For all its appeal, and its pivotal role in the city's history, the sea could not provide one crucial thing, and that was water. The land would have to provide the water, and this land did not have much water to give. The war and a 1940s population surge that boosted the county census from less than 300,000 to over 550,000 brought into keen focus the contradiction of a city with water, water, everywhere, and not many drops to drink.

San Diego's latter-day history, post 1850, is really a history of people devising new and innovative ways to move water over land where wagons and railroads couldn't go. At the time Alonzo Horton, a 19th century businessman, was moving the city's center from Old Town to downtown, residents got their water from wells and a reservoir constructed in Pound Canyon that bisected what was then City Park. Today the park is called Balboa, and Highway 163, San Diego's first freeway, follows the floor of the canyon from Mission Valley to downtown.

The county's 14 dams, among them El Capitan, Barrett, Hodges, and San Vicente, stand now as concrete growth rings marking San Diego's expansion in the 1920s and '30s. But their effectiveness depended on rainfall, always an uncertain event in Southern California. City planners already were looking to the Colorado River to meet future needs. Designs were drawn to lift river water over the mountains from the new All-American Canal in the Imperial Valley.

Then World War II broke, and water for San Diego became a federal issue. San Diego, wanting local control, favored the All-American Canal system but realized construction would take too long. The Metropolitan Aqueduct, bringing Colorado River water through San Gorgonio Pass to the Los Angeles Basin, had been completed in 1941. President Roosevelt in 1944 directed the Navy to build a pipeline to San Diego from the Metropolitan Aqueduct. Ironically, construction began as the war was ending, and the first Colorado River water did not arrive in San Diego until December 1947.

All the same, war had brought to San Diego the last two pieces of a catapult that would propel the city toward the threshold of prominence. One was water, and the other was awareness. All those military people spread the word about San Diego, and many of them came back here to live. In the Eastern media San Diego's image changed from a "sleepy village" to a "sleepy Navy town." Within the decade jet travel would become a reality, and the interstate highway system would finally drive a wide and easy passage through the eastern mountains. After four centuries, San Diego's land gateways were beginning to open.

> **SAN DIEGO'S LATTER-DAY HISTORY, POST 1850, IS REALLY A HISTORY OF PEOPLE DEVISING NEW AND INNOVATIVE WAYS TO MOVE WATER OVER LAND WHERE WAGONS AND RAILROADS COULDN'T GO.**

T HE HISTORIC IRON-HULLED SAILING SHIP *Star of India*
AND THE MOON, BOTH UNDER FULL ILLUMINATION,
COMPETE FOR THE ATTENTION OF STROLLERS ON A
CRYSTALLINE NIGHT ALONG THE Embarcadero.

THE SPANISH FRIARS, WITH FATHER JUNÍPERO SERRA IN THE LEAD, WERE THE FIRST EUROPEAN SETTLERS IN THE SAN DIEGO REGION, ARRIVING HERE IN THE SECOND HALF OF THE 18TH CENTURY AND SETTING STRAIGHT TO THE TASKS OF CONSTRUCTION AND CONVERSION. THEY BUILT THEIR FIRST SAN DIEGO MISSION ON PRESIDIO HILL AND THEN BUILT THE MISSION DE ALCALÁ A FEW MILES EAST IN MISSION VALLEY ON THE SAN DIEGO RIVER.

H ISTORY CAN'T PROVIDE A PORTRAIT OF THE
VERY FIRST HUMAN INHABITANTS OF THE
SAN DIEGO LATITUDES, BUT THE NATIVE
AMERICAN PRESENCE WAS WELL ESTAB-
LISHED IN SOUTHERN CALIFORNIA BY THE
TIME THE EUROPEANS ARRIVED. THE
DIEGUEÑO INDIANS, FOREBEARS OF THIS
FAMILY AS PAINTED BY A MID-19TH
CENTURY ARTIST, GREETED CABRILLO
UPON HIS LANDING IN 1542.

THE BREWSTER FARM, LOCATED IN AN AREA THAT IS NOW
NATIONAL CITY, SHOWS THE EARLY SAN DIEGANS'
AWARENESS OF THE LAND'S AGRICULTURAL POTENTIAL.
THEY SANK WELLS, PUMPED WATER UP WITH WINDMILLS,
AND THEN CHANNELED IT THROUGH ORCHARDS WHICH
THRIVED.

THE SPANIARDS INTRODUCED THE HORSE INTO THE
SOUTHWEST IN THE 1500S. THE ANIMAL QUICKLY
BECAME THE DOMINANT SYMBOL OF SOUTHWESTERN
LIFE, CARRYING A COMPLETE COWBOYS-AND-INDIANS
MYTHOLOGY ON ITS BACK, SO TO SPEAK. THE HORSEMEN
IN THE ETCHING OF MISSION SAN LUIS REY ARE
PURSUING THE AGES-OLD "CHICKEN-PULL" SPORT.

S AN DIEGO CULTURAL AND SOCIAL LIFE IN THE 18TH AND 19TH CENTURIES WAS TYPICAL OF A SOUTHWESTERN BORDER TOWN. A PAINTING FROM THE ERA SHOWS A LIVELY GATHERING HIGHLIGHTED BY THE FANDANGO, A SPANISH-AMERICAN DANCE POPULAR IN FRONTIER REGIONS.

A MAP MADE IN 1782 BY SHIP PILOT JUAN PANTOJA SHOWS THE DISTINCTIVE POINT LOMA PROMONTORY AND THE U-SHAPED NATURAL HARBOR HAILED BY SPANISH EXPLORERS AS AMONG THE FINEST IN THE SOUTH SEAS. MISSION BAY, THEN CALLED "FALSE BAY," IS CHARTED ALONG WITH THE PRESIDIO MISSION FOUNDED BY JUNÍPERO SERRA IN 1769. MOST IMPORTANT TO PANTOJA, HOWEVER, WERE THE NUMBERS ON THE WATER SHOWING DEPTH SOUNDINGS.

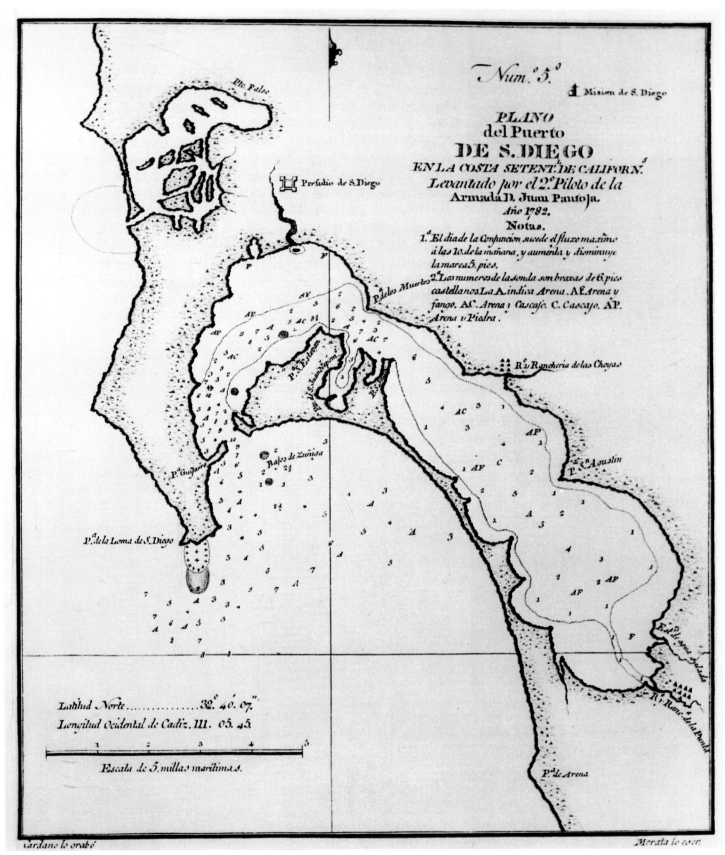

Num.º 5.º

⚓ Mision de S. Diego

PLANO
del Puerto
DE S. DIEGO
EN LA COSTA SETENT.ᴰᴱ DE CALIFORN.ˢ
Levantado por el 2.º Piloto de la
Armada D. Juan Pantoja.
Año 1782.
Notas.
1.ª El dia de la Conjuncion sucede el fluxo maximo
á las 10. de la mañana, y aumenta y diminuye
la marea 5. pies.
2.ª Los numeros de la sonda son brazas de 6. pies
castellanos La A. indica Arena. AF. Arena y
fango. AC. Arena y Cascajo. C. Cascajo. AP.
Arena y Piedra .

Pta Falsa

Presidio de S. Diego

Pᵗᵃ de los Muertes

R.ᵃ y Rancheria de las Choyas

Pᵗᵃ S.ⁿ Agustin

Pˢ. Guijaros

Pᵗᵃ de la Loma de S. Diego

Bajos de Zuñiga

Pᵗᵃ de Arena

Latitud Norte . . . . 32.º 40. 07."
Longitud Ocidental de Cadiz. III. 05. 45.

Escala de 5. millas maritimas.

Cardano lo grabó

Morata lo eser.

A statue of San Diego's first European visitor, Juan Rodriguez Cabrillo, shares a spectacular view from Point Loma with several more recent arrivals. (Previous Pages)
Jerry Rife photo

The National City & Otay Railroad connected San Diego with Tijuana in the 1880s. San Diego boosters in the 19th century tied their hopes for the city's future to a railroad that would link up with transcontinental lines approaching from the east. But the nearby mountains were difficult to cross, and the builders chose a more accessible route to the north into Los Angeles.

I
N 1895, THE STEAMSHIP WHARF AREA WAS AN ACTIVE
CENTER OF TRADE AND COMMERCE, AS WELL AS RECREA-
TION. THE WHITE BUILDINGS ON STILTS ARE THE SAN
DIEGO ROWING CLUB, AND AT THE FAR RIGHT OF THE
PHOTOGRAPH IS THE SANTA FE WHARF.

This is the corner of Fifth Avenue and C Street downtown in 1903. Updated versions of the horseless carriage still pass by the corner in greater and greater numbers, and after an absence of several decades the trolley tracks are back. But horse-and-buggies are a rare sight except on balmy evenings around the Embarcadero, Harbor Drive, and Seaport Village.

S AN DIEGO'S COLORFUL AVIATION HISTORY INCLUDES NAVY PARACHUTISTS JUMPING FROM WINGTIPS ACCORDING TO STANDARD MILITARY PROCEDURES IN USE IN 1928. NORTH ISLAND IS BELOW, POINT LOMA IN THE DISTANCE. NAVY DIRIGIBLES ALSO HAD THEIR DAY IN SAN DIEGO; PICTURED HERE IS A C-6 MODEL BEING REMOVED FROM ITS NORTH ISLAND HANGER IN PREPARATION FOR LAUNCHING IN THE EARLY 1920S.

ST. LOUIS MAIL PILOT CHARLES A. LINDBERGH CAME TO SAN DIEGO IN EARLY 1927 BECAUSE OF A RYAN AIRPLANE COMPANY ADVERTISEMENT IN A TRADE JOURNAL. LINDBERGH WANTED TO BE THE FIRST TO FLY NON-STOP FROM NEW YORK TO PARIS, AND HE THOUGHT THE ADVERTISED RYAN MONOPLANE MIGHT BE THE DESIGN TO DO IT. RYAN BUILT THE PLANE IN 60 DAYS, AND ON MAY 20-21, 1927, LINDBERGH FLEW IT INTO HISTORY.

CHOICES
FROM
THE PRESENT

MOST OF THE COUNTRY DOES NOT REALIZE WHAT KIND OF COMMITMENT IT TAKES TO LIVE IN SAN DIEGO. THE CITY GETS HIT WITH THESE RAGING WINTER SUN STORMS, AND YET EVERYBODY GETS TO WORK. ◆ DO SAN DIEGANS GET AN OUNCE OF CREDIT FOR IT? HECK, NO. IN FEBRUARY EVERY YEAR, THE PAPERS WILL HAVE TWO OR THREE BIG STORIES ABOUT SNOWSTORMS IN THE EAST, STORMS THAT HAVE PARALYZED BOSTON, NEW YORK, AND PHILADELPHIA, AND EVERYONE STAYS HOME FROM WORK. FINE FOR THEM. NOBODY BEGRUDGES THESE EASTERNERS A COUPLE OF DAYS OFF, SNUGGLED AT HOME BY THE FIRE WITH A GOOD BOOK. ◆ AT THAT SAME TIME, A RIDGE OF HIGH PRESSURE WILL SETTLE OVER THE SOUTHWEST, BLOCKING OUT THE RAINY WINTER FRONTS THAT WANT TO COME DOWN THE COAST FROM ALASKA. THE HIGH PRESSURE SPINS WARM AIR OFF THE DESERTS OVER THE MOUNTAINS INTO SOUTHERN CALIFORNIA. A SAN DIEGAN CALLS THIS CONDITION A "SANTA ANNA," AND HE CAN SENSE ONE COMING WHEN HE GOES OUT FOR THE PAPER IN THE MORNING. ◆ IT MAY BE BARELY DAWN, BUT HE WILL FEEL A DISTINCTIVE WARMTH IN THE AIR, AND THERE MAY BE A BREATH OF BREEZE FROM THE EAST. THE SKY WILL BE CRYSTAL CLEAR, AND THE STARFIELD WILL SEEM CLOSE, LIKE A DESERT SKY. ◆ "UH OH," HE WILL SAY. "SUN STORM COMING." ◆ SURE ENOUGH, BY 7 A.M. ON THIS FEBRUARY MORNING, THE TEMPERATURE MAY ALREADY HAVE HIT 70°, AND EVERY FEATURE OF THE LAND WILL BE FLOODED BY THE PARTICULARLY GOLDEN SUNLIGHT OF WINTER. THE SAN DIEGAN WILL SIT ON THE PATIO, DRINKING COFFEE AND READING ABOUT ALL THE EASTERNERS STAYING HOME FROM WORK, AND IT WILL GIVE HIM IDEAS ABOUT CALLING THE OFFICE AND SAYING, "LISTEN, I DON'T THINK I CAN DRIVE THROUGH ALL THIS SUNLIGHT." ◆ THEN HE COULD STAY AT HOME, HAVE A LATE BREAKFAST, PUTTER AROUND THE YARD, TEND THE FLOWER BEDS, GET A LITTLE TAN, TAKE A NAP IN THE SWING, MAYBE PLAY SOME GOLF IN THE AFTERNOON. ◆ BUT HE WON'T. HE WILL GET DRESSED AND DRIVE TO WORK, AS WILL ALL—WELL, ALMOST ALL—SAN DIEGANS, SUN POURING

A high-rise condo, sparkling pool, Spanish tile, California girl, fashion swimwear, plenty of sunscreen, a day that could belong to July or January—all making a statement about the paradise that is San Diego. (Jerry Rife photo)

down, streaming in through their open car windows and blanketing the hills and valleys with warmth.

It is ridiculous, trying to go to work on a February day like that. But San Diegans do. They gird their loins and go, because they know there is the Gross National Product to think of.

Do they ever get a headline in the Eastern press? "Sun storm buries San Diego; everyone gets to work." It'll never happen.

But word trickles back. The Chamber of Commerce receives regular queries from Easterners who ask, tentatively, as if convinced someone was pulling their leg, about the story their neighbors told, the ones who just got back from a convention in San Diego and insisted they saw people mowing their lawns in January.

And they see San Diego on television, as television follows the winter professional golf tour. The PGA has a pair of stops in San Diego: the Tournament of Champions at La Costa and the Put Your Company's Name Here Andy Williams San Diego Open (the sponsorship has had a habit of changing) at Torrey Pines. The no-growthers in San Diego always pray for rain, wind, cold, any combination of weather giving the appearance of misery, at the time of these January and February tournaments. Then when the weekend of the final rounds dawns bright and sunny, and television sends back pictures of the green Torrey Pines circuit on the bluffs above the blue Pacific, and viewers learn that it is a municipal course, and the television blimp shows pictures of business as usual going on in San Diego in spite of pouring-down sun, why, a viewer in Ohio may feel stirring within him a new sense of purpose.

After an hour or two of watching human beings walking around outside in January in shorts and pullovers, he may suddenly throw off his lap robes, and, rising to his feet, eyes ablaze with commitment as he stares at the figures on the screen, stab a gloved, trembling finger into the air and cry, "I can do that!"

It happens all the time. The hide-a-bed and roll-a-way rental bed industries in San Diego are recession-proof. Easterners make the San Diego commitment, relocate here, and within six weeks receive word from relatives and friends back East that they are coming for a visit. The newcomers first rent a roll-a-way, but eventually invest in the hide-a-bed, because the visits from back East tend to become regular to the point that the relatives start to look like furniture.

The newcomers are naturally eager to show off their adopted city, but this takes time. Their first sight-seeing trips hit the high spots: Balboa Park, the San Diego Zoo, the Wild Animal Park, Old Town, the Hotel del Coronado (a favorite but debunked legend says Prince Edward first met Wallis Warfield Simpson there), Tijuana, the beaches, and the Padres in season.

The astute relative from the East will notice that with each successive visit his hosts are showing him the city in greater depth. Getting to know San Diego is a progressive feast that goes forward on its own unhurried terms. It has a curious effect on new residents, who may notice after their arrival that the "settled-in" feeling is slow to come. It may take years. A Texan, relocating to San Diego in 1972, found that it was about 1980 before he felt "at home" here. Of course, Texans are slow to let go. New Yorkers,

> THE HIDE-A-BED AND ROLL-A-WAY RENTAL BED INDUSTRIES IN SAN DIEGO ARE RECESSION-PROOF. EASTERNERS MAKE THE SAN DIEGO COMMITMENT, RELOCATE HERE, AND WITHIN SIX WEEKS RECEIVE WORD FROM RELATIVES AND FRIENDS BACK EAST THAT THEY ARE COMING FOR A VISIT.

whose narcissism tends to be unparalleled, are even worse. New Yorkers making the San Diego adjustment have been heard to paraphrase Gertrude Stein's famous line about Oakland: "There is no *there* there." In fact, in San Diego the case is just the opposite: there is *so much there* here.

Eventually, newcomers discover that San Diego simply has a different root system. The typical Eastern and Midwestern system is a traditional community taproot that goes deep and is easy to find. San Diego, however, is a place of vast options, in topography and philosophy, in vocations and avocations, in art and in leisure, in substance and in style. Runners shoot out laterally like Bermuda grass, passing up some options, attaching to others, sometimes consciously, sometimes unconsciously. Then one day it comes to a person, usually in a flash of realization, that his San Diego roots are in. The Texan, for example, recalls that this surprising sense of certification came to him one beautiful October morning in 1981 when, with 3,000 or 4,000 other people, he ran a 10-kilometer race from Coronado across the Bay Bridge to the finish line at the handsome County Administration Center on Harbor Drive. The bridge was closed to traffic for the event, which benefited the Heart Association, and, as he arrived at the crest of the graceful, curving bridge—the harbor and downtown skyline on the left, the shipyards and mountains and Mexico on the right, the sweat of participation all around him—he suddenly felt very San Diegan.

When that happens, all of a sudden a pattern becomes evident in San Diego's enormous complexity, like threads merging into a tapestry that reveals a newly woven map of the world.

LIVING IN SAN DIEGO IS LIKE WAKING UP EVERY MORNING AT THE STARTING POINT OF AN ODYSSEY. THE SIREN SONGS COME FROM ALL DIRECTIONS.

Living in San Diego is like waking up every morning at the starting point of an odyssey. The siren songs come from all directions. The odyssey can begin anywhere, on any given day, but an ideal time is, perhaps, a Thursday in late January. The hero of this journey should be at the office, but with cellular phone contact, what the heck. He tells the boss he'll be "in the field, doing research."

He begins at the Cabrillo National Monument, at the tip of Point Loma, standing at the sandstone feet of the discoverer himself. There is among San Diegans an unresolved debate over the choice between "Cabree-o," the Spanish pronounciation, and "Cabrillo," (rhyming with "Brillo") which is the Portuguese pronunciation. Whichever, the gentleman from his promontory has an astonishing view. John Nolen, a nationally known city planner of the early 1900s, stood on this spot and called it "one of the most remarkable views in the accessible world." It is a view of the ocean, and the harbor entrance (through which, this being an ideal day, the aircraft carrier *Ranger* steams with colors flying) and North Island and Coronado beyond, and downtown at the harbor bend, and the coastal plain rising to the foothills and the eastern mountains. The tallest of these, Laguna and Cuyamaca, appear white this morning because last night a winter storm passed through bringing rain to the coast and dropping the snow level to 3,000 feet. This morning on Point Loma the air is brisk—50 degrees, say—and the sky, a startling blue, brings all of San Diego's man-made and geographic definitions into sharp focus.

The traveler can't do it all in a day, but he can take notes as he goes. He heads north first, looping past the historic old lighthouse at the base of the point, then past the green fields of Fort Rosecrans National Cemetery, its serene ranks of white headstones overlooking the harbor. Then a turn down the windward side of the point reveals Sunset Cliffs and Ocean Beach. It's a good morning for the surfers. People who have an image of surfers as tanned, bleached-blond boys of summer should come down to Sunset Cliffs and South Mission Beach and La Jolla Shores in winter. The storms coming off the ocean create a surge that means good surf. People curious enough to visit the beach before dawn will see the surfers in their black wet suits, cruising the beachfront streets in their vans, VWs, and pickup trucks, peering through the darkness (and, sometimes, the pouring rain) at the white surf, gauging it, picking the time and place to get the boards off the roof and paddle out through the rain and the cold. They will surf until it's time to go to school or work. People passing by later in the day will see many of them still out there, and it inspires the landlubber to push on to the Pannikin in La Jolla for *café au lait*. The route north from Ocean Beach crosses the mouth of the San Diego River and makes the Ingraham Avenue traverse across Mission Bay.

Even with their roots in, San Diegans still get a sense, whenever they pass by Mission Bay, of what a very long way this place is from Texas or Missouri or Ohio. Mission Bay, once called False Bay, epitomizes what the civic mind can do, especially when bent on creating real estate.

PEOPLE CURIOUS ENOUGH TO VISIT THE BEACH BEFORE DAWN WILL SEE THE SURFERS IN THEIR BLACK WET SUITS, CRUISING THE BEACHFRONT STREETS IN THEIR VANS, VWs, AND PICKUP TRUCKS, PEERING THROUGH THE DARKNESS (AND, SOMETIMES, THE POURING RAIN) AT THE WHITE SURF, GAUGING IT, PICKING THE TIME AND PLACE TO GET THE BOARDS OFF THE ROOF AND PADDLE OUT THROUGH THE RAIN AND THE COLD.

Dredging, channeling, island-building, and balanced planning have turned what was mostly mud flats into a sheltered aquatic paradise. The tall tower marks Sea World, the original, which calls for its own tour another day. Beyond Sea World lies man-made Fiesta Island, which remains barren and unimproved, though it is the site of one of summer's more remarkable events in San Diego or anywhere else. The World Championship of Over-The-Line or "OTL," as San Diegans call it, is a kind of three-person softball game that the 1,000-odd participating teams take very seriously. But that is the only thing taken seriously on the island during the two July weekends of the tournament. The players—doctors, dentists, lawyers, accountants, bankers, executives, family men and women—dote on clever team names that usually can't be printed in the newspaper, and all the lady spectators' swim wear taken together wouldn't provide yardage for a decent place mat. A person who has been to OTL, when he tells of it back home, will dwell on the spectators, and the worship of sun, fun, and irreverence, and the annual competition to select "Ms. Emerson," the OTL queen whose title is a contraction of the words "Them are some." Then at the end of the story he'll get around to the game's legitimacy and the intensity with which it is played, which is the way *Sports Illustrated* featured the championship a few seasons back.

On the left, visible from Ingraham Avenue, is the old Belmont Park roller coaster at Mission

Beach, the largest wooden roller coaster in the world. Its restoration took years of volunteer love, and, in 1991, the completed project won an Orchid in the city's annual "Orchids and Onions" architectural competition. From Mission Bay to Pacific Beach to La Jolla are the prime areas where international jet-setters keep second (and sometimes first) homes with stupendous views of the long crescent shoreline. The Salk Institute, one of the world's ranking research and architectural marvels, is on the route. At the top of Torrey Pines Road, the drive winds through the campus of the University of California at San Diego, where the faculty has included as many as eight Nobel laureates and whose physics students every spring hold the Watermelon Drop competitions from the top of Urey Hall. The winning watermelon is that with the greatest blast radius.

North of UC San Diego, on bluffs high above the Pacific, is Torrey Pines State Park, one of only two sites in the world where the rare Torrey Pine is found. The groves and land were dedicated to the city in the 1920s by Ellen Browning Scripps, half-sister of the newspaper publisher, whose philanthropical support of the city is readily apparent (the Zoo, Balboa Park, Natural History Museum, Scripps Institution) to this day.

At Del Mar the odyssey turns inland at the racetrack and fairgrounds, home each June to the Southern California Exposition, which everybody calls the "Del Mar Fair." The thoroughbred racing season begins in July and runs into September, drawing daily attendance of over 20,000. In 1991, the Del Mar Turf Club set new records for its wagering "handle," staged its first million-dollar race, the Pacific Cup, and began a complete renovation of the main grandstand. The Volvo Cup, the world's ranking equestrian jumping event, is booked for 1992 at the new stadium completed on the grounds in 1991.

A group headed by crooner Bing Crosby built the track in 1937, and before each day's races the track's anthem, sung by Crosby, rises above the grandstand:

"Where the turf meets the surf, down at old Del Mar, Take a train, take a plane, take a car ... "

There is a story, possibly apocryphal but favored by San Diegans, that "White Christmas,— the best-selling song of all time (eat your heart out, San Francisco), is San Diego's official song. It makes sense. Irving Berlin wrote "White Christmas" and Crosby introduced it in the 1942 movie *Holiday Inn*. The story was set in New England, but the truth is those gentlemen knew it was San Diego's song all along. Crosby, particularly, had spent a lot of time here and knew that this city was the White Christmas-dreaming capital of the world. It still is, even more so. In downtown San Diego, for example, it is obviously the Christmas season when December arrives and workers go to lunch at some sunny sidewalk cafe with vacant looks on their faces. They came from Ohio, Michigan, and Pennsylvania, and they are dreaming about a White Christmas, just like the ones they used to know. Irving Berlin, no dummy, knew it was

> **AT THE TOP OF TORREY PINES ROAD, THE DRIVE WINDS THROUGH THE CAMPUS OF THE UNIVERSITY OF CALIFORNIA AT SAN DIEGO, WHERE THE FACULTY HAS INCLUDED AS MANY AS EIGHT NOBEL LAUREATES AND WHOSE PHYSICS STUDENTS EVERY SPRING HOLD THE WATERMELON DROP COMPETITIONS FROM THE TOP OF UREY HALL. THE WINNING WATERMELON IS THAT WITH THE GREATEST BLAST RADIUS.**

unlikely Pennsylvanians could sing "White Christmas," with five feet of snow on the ground, with anything resembling the authenticity of the lyric as sung in San Diego.

To the left, which is north on Interstate 5, are the flower fields at Carlsbad, a year-round source of fresh flowers for the nation, and the resort at La Costa. Farther north are the beach amenities in Laguna Beach and Newport Beach, and, beyond that, Disneyland, about a 90-minute trip depending on traffic. But this is a San Diego odyssey, and in order to be back in the city for dinner, the traveler wants to continue east on Via de la Valle, through groves of oak and eucalyptus, past Fairbanks Ranch, the site of the equestrian events in the 1984 Olympics. Among the residents of Fairbanks Ranch is Joan Kroc, whose modern-day philanthropy in San Diego and elsewhere echoes that of Ellen Browning Scripps. Mrs. Kroc is the widow of Ray Kroc, founder of the McDonald's hamburger chain, who became a San Diego hero in 1974 by buying the Padres when it appeared the team was destined to be sold to another city.

The Padres weren't very good in those days, and Kroc made another career mark one night at Jack Murphy Stadium. Near the end of another Padres loss, he marched into the public address booth, seized the microphone from a very startled announcer, apologized to the equally startled fans, and told them, "I've never seen such stupid ball-playing in my life." Kroc died early in 1984, the same year his Padres won the National League pennant and brought the World Series (versus the Detroit Tigers) to Mission Valley.

A GROUP HEADED BY CROONER BING CROSBY BUILT THE DEL MAR TURF CLUB IN 1937, AND BEFORE EACH DAY'S RACES THE TRACK'S ANTHEM, SUNG BY CROSBY, RISES ABOVE THE GRANDSTAND: "WHERE THE TURF MEETS THE SURF, DOWN AT OLD DEL MAR, TAKE A TRAIN, TAKE A PLANE, TAKE A CAR ... "

To the east, the terrain changes quickly from coastal plain to steep foothill slopes, and the ubiquitous gray-green latticework is actually grove after grove of avocado trees. The trees like the slopes because their root systems can suffer from standing water, and their effect on the landscape (and the county's economy) is pleasant. The stands of oak become denser, and, at this time of year, the slopes and canyons are fuzzy-green with the winter rains.

If the traveler angles north on Highway S6, he can buzz up Palomar Mountain to visit the observatory and its 200-inch telescope. Angling south, he crosses high meadow country to the thriving back-country community of Ramona. The temperature is dropping now because the terrain is gaining altitude. Beyond Ramona is the village of Santa Ysabel, where the faithful always stop at Dudley's Bakery for the obligatory fresh-baked loaves of white and wheat and jalapeno cheese bread. A long, pastoral highway leaves Santa Ysabel through a valley to the north, passing the Santa Ysabel Mission en route to the high pastureland around Warner Hot Springs. But this odyssey continues east, up the mountain to Julian, beneath a residual cloud canopy from the departing storm. It is cold now, car-heater cold, and the evergreen forest and apple orchards are dusted with snow. Julian, an old gold-mining town, is famous for its apples and its flannel-shirt atmosphere. The tour stops at one of the several country stores on the winding highway west of town for a half-gallon of fresh-squeezed cider off the back of a truck to be drunk ice cold, straight from the jug.

In town, Julian residents and visitors are walking in a winter wonderland. On a day like this after a cold cider aperitif, Julian may be, paraphrasing city planner John Nolen, "one of the most remarkable stops for lunch in the accessible world." Lunch may be chicken or chili, but it will finish with a piece of apple pie in a storybook crust, warmed in the oven with a covering wedge of cheddar.

Half an hour later, after a sharp, winding descent down the Banner Grade, the traveler arrives at the floor of the great Colorado Desert that stretches east 125 miles to the Colorado River. Six hours ago he was sipping *cafe au lait* in a jeweled community by the sea. Now he is on the rugged perimeter of a low desert that at El Centro dips below sea level. Down here the day is clear and warm. Behind him clouds cling to the line of mountains that funneled the early explorers and settlers north to the Los Angeles basin. Ahead, further east, are the desert resort and recreational opportunities around Borrego Springs. All around are the desert flora, particularly tall stalks of ocotillo cactus that in March or maybe April will bloom in a profusion that draws San Diegans by the thousands to a tour of the desert.

A good, scenic county highway angles southeast for 60 miles across the Anza-Borrego Desert State Park to Interstate 8. But today the trip will go the short way, back up the Banner Grade, because tonight there is an opportunity for theater tickets in town, or maybe symphony tickets, or opera tickets, or hockey tickets. Back at Julian, the route turns south through the mountain campground and lake areas of Cuyamaca State Park. Even on a Thursday the highway is lined with the parked cars of San Diegans who have come up with their kids to enjoy the high altitude and to play in the strange cold white stuff. The mountain road connects with Interstate 8 at the crest of a long descent back to the coastal plain. On the way, the highway offers a sweeping view of the Pacific and, standing out in crystal clarity, the Coronado Islands.

Back in town, choices abound. The museums and galleries are closed by now, but things to do—theater, dance, music, clubs, sports—fill a whole page of listings in the Friday *San Diego Union-Tribune*. On any given night this week there may be a touring Broadway show at the Civic Theater, a national dance troupe at the Spreckels, Mozart at Copley Symphony Hall, new plays with Broadway potential at the Old Globe or La Jolla Playhouse, "Greater Tuna" at the Lyceum, hockey or rock-and-roll at the Sports Arena. Later in the spring and summer, people can consider outdoor stages at the Old Globe and Starlight and the summer Pops series at Embarcadero Marina Park. They can stroll Seaport Village at the Embarcadero or browse in Horton Plaza. They can stop in for a drink at Mr. A's, the aerie atop the Fifth Avenue Financial Center, with its close view of Balboa Park and downtown and the harbor and Point Loma and the airliners gliding past toward their Lindbergh Field touchdowns. On board are passengers flying in from all over the country who didn't see any more in their intercontinental sojourns than did the traveler in today's odyssey. Tomorrow the siren songs will come again. But tomorrow is a workday, sun storm or no.

> SIX HOURS AGO, THE TRAVELER WAS SIPPING CAFE AU LAIT IN A JEWELED COMMUNITY BY THE SEA. NOW HE IS ON THE RUGGED PERIMETER OF A LOW DESERT THAT, AT EL CENTRO, DIPS BELOW SEA LEVEL.... ALL AROUND ARE THE DESERT FLORA, PARTICULARLY TALL STALKS OF OCOTILLO CACTUS THAT IN MARCH OR MAYBE APRIL WILL BLOOM IN A PROFUSION THAT DRAWS SAN DIEGANS BY THE THOUSANDS TO A TOUR OF THE DESERT.

Southern California in the second half of the 20th century has developed a reputation for glitz and glitter that cannot be denied. But away from the neon is found a profile, like this one of Balboa Park's California Tower, that tells the greater truth about California, truth rooted in a spirit for the ages, surpassing any fashion of the moment.

T HE DOWNTOWN SKYLINE IS RESHAPED IN THE CLEAN-EDGED, HIGH-PROFILE VISION OF AN APPROACHING NEW CENTURY, AND BRAND NEW SKYLINES ARE RISING IN MISSION VALLEY AND THE GOLDEN TRIANGLE. SAN DIEGO IS PREPARING TO COME INTO HER OWN ON THE NATIONAL AND INTERNATIONAL STAGE, AND WITH THOSE EXPECTATIONS COMES THE SAME KIND OF IMPATIENCE THAT YOUNG MEN FEEL WATCHING FOR THE NEXT GOOD SET OF WAVES. EVERYONE KNOWS THEY WILL COME, BUT WHEN?

A T THE 1991 PGA TOURNAMENT OF CHAMPIONS AT LA COSTA, CHI CHI RODRIGUEZ ASSUMED THE DOGLEG-LEFT POSITION IN SUPPORT OF A PUTT THAT APPARENTLY HAD OTHER DIRECTIONAL IDEAS. THE NATIONAL TELEVISION AUDIENCE MAY NOT HAVE SEEN THIS PARTICULAR JUXTAPOSITION OF WILLS, BUT VIEWERS BACK EAST SEE ENOUGH OF SAN DIEGO'S ANNUAL WINTER PGA EVENTS AT LA COSTA AND TORREY PINES TO DEVELOP A GRUDGE AGAINST PEOPLE WHO CAN PLAY 18 IN JANUARY.

S AN DIEGANS TEND TO ENJOY FITNESS AND TO PREFER PARTICI- PATORY SPORTS. HARDLY A WEEK- END PASSES THAT A 10-K RUN OR A BIKE TOUR OR A SOFT-DRINK- CUP SLALOM IS NOT BEING SET UP SOMEWHERE. THE INDIVIDUAL PICTURED LOOKS TO BE A CON- TENDER FOR TOP MONEY IN THE 55-GOING-ON-18 DIVISION, WITH EXCELLENT FORM GOING INTO THE MOUNTAIN DEW GATE AND ALL CUPS IN THE COURSE STILL STANDING. ESPN DID NOT COVER THE EVENT, BUT THIS IS A NEW SPORT, STILL CATCHING ON.

SAN DIEGO ENJOYS OCEAN SPORTS ON THE WEST SIDE, MOUNTAIN SPORTS ON THE EAST SIDE, AND SEVERAL LAND VERSIONS IN BETWEEN. WHEN SOME INVENTIVE YOUNG CALIFORNIAN GOT THE IDEA TO PUT A SURFBOARD ON WHEELS, THE ENERGETIC WATER SPORT CAME UP ONTO LAND TO BECOME SKATEBOARDING. IT NEVER SNOWS IN SAN DIEGO — WELL, ONCE IN A BLUE MOON — BUT THERE ARE GRASSY SLOPES AND ROLLER-SKIS ON WHICH TO

PRACTICE FOR THE REAL THING, WHICH, WHEN THE WINTER SNOWS COME, IS ONLY TWO OR THREE HOURS AWAY. SAN DIEGO COUNTY'S LAGUNA MOUNTAINS AREN'T HIGH OR STEEP ENOUGH TO SUPPORT A SKIING INDUSTRY, BUT WHEN THE SNOW LEVEL DROPS TO 3,000 FEET, SAN DIEGANS FLOCK WITH SLEDS AND TRASH-CAN LIDS TO THE LAGUNA "SLOPES."

WHERE THERE IS SUN, THERE WILL BE A BENCH, OR IN THIS CASE, HANDSOME WROUGHT-IRON CHAIRS ALONG THE PRADO IN BALBOA PARK. (PREVIOUS PAGES) THE ARCHITECTS WHO DESIGNED THE PARK KNEW THAT THEIR COLUMNS WOULD NOT ONLY HOLD UP ARCADES, BUT ALSO GIVE BACK SUPPORT TO GENERATIONS OF STROLLERS (AND BIKERS) PAUSING A MOMENT TO TAKE IN THE SUN. *Jerry Rife photo*

WHEN SAN DIEGO BOOSTERS CONCEIVED A PACIFIC-PANAMA EXPOSITION AND PUT UP THE BUILDINGS TO HOUSE THE EXPOSITION IN 1915, BALBOA PARK ACQUIRED ITS LIFELONG CHARACTER. OVER THE YEARS, RECONSTRUCTIONS AND ADDITIONS HAVE RESURRECTED BUILDINGS THAT WERE LOST IN TRAGIC FIRES; SOME STRUCTURES REQUIRE RENOVATION STILL, SIMPLY FROM THE RIGORS OF OLD AGE. BUT THE PARK, PICTURES OF WHOSE FOUNTAINS AND FACADES HAVE CIRCULATED WORLDWIDE ON THE BACKS OF MILLIONS OF POSTCARDS, WILL FOREVER RETAIN ITS ROMANTIC SPANISH-AMERICAN AMBIANCE.

Dr. Seuss, or Ted Geisel, as his La Jolla neighbors knew him, would have applauded a property owner's decision to paint his exteriors red and white, or black and blue, if that looked right. He thought tall about walls, especially walls that said all, since the wall, as it went, took with it the eye to the start of the sky. That's no apparition on the Museum of Art; it's the Cat in the Hat, perched there at a show of Seussian art.

THE ARCHITECTURE OF THE EXPOSITION BUILDINGS IN BALBOA PARK TWISTS LIGHT INTO ROMANTIC STATUARY AND BAROQUE BREAD-STICK COLUMNS ACROSS THE FRONT OF THE MUSEUM OF MAN, THEN ELSEWHERE BENDS IT INTO THE PRECISE GEOMETRY OF ARCHES AND VAULTS, AN EXPRESSION OF ART AT ITS MOST INTELLEC- TUAL AND SELF-ASSURED.

Some of our animal friends know where they are going, some would like to know more, and others appear content to contemplate the here-and-now. One never has to wonder about dogs, but then there's Gordon, a year-old gorilla at the time of this shot, who hasn't quite grasped the idea that he is being delivered in limousine style from his old home at the San Diego Zoo to new turf at the San Diego Wild Animal Park. The other fella? Well, if it's Tuesday, these must be Belgians.

THE WILD ANIMAL PARK WAS OPENED IN THE 1970S TO
PROVIDE CAPTIVE ANIMALS AN ENVIRONMENT MORE
REPRESENTATIVE OF LIFE IN THE WILD. THE PARK
CERTAINLY GIVES THE ANIMALS MORE ROOM TO STRETCH
THEIR LEGS. IT IS QUITE A PERK FOR THE GIRAFFES, WHO
HAVE THE RUN (REMOVED, OF COURSE, FROM THE
BIG-CAT ENCLOSURES) OF THE SPRAWLING PRESERVE IN
THE SAN PASQUAL VALLEY.

T HE ADVANTAGE OF SPACE AT THE WILD ANIMAL PARK
BENEFITS HUMANS AS WELL AS ANIMALS. VISITORS PROFIT
FROM PERSPECTIVES THAT RANGE FROM LONG VIEWS TO
MIDDLE DISTANCE GLIMPSES, THE LATTER BEING THE
MOST EXCITING OF ALL—MORE LIKE BOUNCING ALONG A
ROAD IN THE SAVANNA AND SUDDENLY SPOTTING ELE-
PHANTS AT PLAY IN A COPSE OF TREES.

T HE SAN DIEGO ZOO'S BIG, BEAUTIFUL CATS PROBABLY DON'T CARE ANY MORE OR LESS THAN THE ORDINARY HOUSE CAT IF HUMANS ARE WATCHING. THEIR STRENGTH AND GRACE GIVE THEM THE APPEARANCE OF PERPETUALLY POSING FOR THE CAMERAS. ELEPHANTS, ON THE OTHER HAND, FOR ALL THEIR BULK AND BRUTISH APPEAL, SEEM SHY BY COMPARISON.

ABIGAIL KURTZ MAHONEY

LOUISE A. PALAZOLA

At the Zoo the animals exhibit all their fine adaptations to nature. The iguana, sizing up physiologist Andy Phillips' haircut, puts up a picket fence of fins down its back to radiate heat and keep cool. The baby snow leopard puts out its own spiky silhouette to keep heat in.

I N TERMS OF TOPICAL ZONES, SOUTHERN CALIFORNIA IS
OFFICIALLY AN ARID TO SEMI-ARID DESERT, THOUGH THE
STORY GOES THAT ANYTHING WILL GROW HERE IF
WATERED. BALBOA PARK EXHIBITS SPECIMENS FROM ALL
THE COMPASS POINTS, INCLUDING A TROPICAL LILY POND.

AND SPEAKING OF PONDS, CREATIVE MINDS FROM MARK
TWAIN TO E.B. WHITE HAVE HAD SOME FINE THINGS TO
SAY ABOUT FROGS. MAYBE THEY ARE ADMIRED FOR
TURNING A HOMELY APPEARANCE TO AMIABLE EFFECT.
MAYBE IT IS THEIR SONG, WHICH SUGGESTS WARM
AFTERNOONS ON LAZY BAYOUS. MAYBE IT IS THE
SPONTANEITY OF THEIR LOCOMOTION. WHATEVER,
EVERY LILY POND SHOULD HAVE ONE.

Visitors to the seashore, such as this stretch at La Jolla, can depend on encountering some strange creatures. This is as true from the human's perspective as from the crab's.(Previous page) *Abigail Kurtz Mahony photo*

The West Coast of the United States angles southwest in such a way that the San Diego County coast becomes "tucked under," away from the brunt of most of the Pacific storms. Times and tides will come, however, when the surf rises to lash the southern coastline and rout visitors from the rocky point at La Jolla Cove.

THE PICTURESQUE STRETCHES OF COASTLINE IN SAN DIEGO COUNTY ARE THOSE WHERE THE SURF, CASCADING UP IN WHITE SPRAYS FROM THE AQUAMARINE SEA, MEETS A PROFUSION OF YELLOW AND PURPLE SPRAYS, SUCCULENT BLOOMS IN THEIR EMERALD BLANKETS, CASCADING DOWN FROM THE ROCKS. THIS PARTICULAR HAPPY MARRIAGE OF LAND AND SEA IS AT LA JOLLA COVE.

THE OCEAN DOES MUCH TO DEFINE SOUTHERN CALIFORNIA, GEOGRAPHICALLY, ARCHITECTURALLY, CULTURALLY, AND ECONOMICALLY. SURFERS ARE DRAWN — 365 DAYS A YEAR, RAIN OR SHINE — TO THE PULSING ENERGY WHERE WAVES MEET THE SHORE. THE AGE OF AVIATION HAS PROVIDED SAN DIEGANS A BIRD'S-EYE VIEW OF JUST HOW GRAND THEIR COASTLINE IS. ALONG ITS DRAMATIC BEACHES, COSMOPOLITAN COASTAL COMMUNITIES SUCH AS LA JOLLA PROVIDE HOTELS FROM WHOSE PAVILIONS THE OCEAN VIEW IS STUNNING.

SAN DIEGO UNION TRIBUNE / DON KOHLBAUER

69

T HE STUDY OF OCEAN LIFE GOES ON IN VARIED VENUES AROUND SAN DIEGO. A TROUPE OF KILLER WHALES, HEADLINED BY SHAMU, PERFORMS FOR LARGE AUDIENCES AT SEA WORLD, SAN DIEGO'S MA-RINE ZOOLOGICAL PARK. OFF-SHORE, MEANWHILE, INTREPID BI-OLOGISTS MOVE IN, APPROPRIATELY CLOTHED IN METAL MESH GAUNT-LETS, FOR A CLOSER LOOK AT THE BEHAVIOR PATTERNS OF SHARKS.

DON KOHLBAUER

SAN DIEGO UNION TRIBUNE / J. T. MacMILLAN

SAN DIEGO'S HARBOR PROVIDES AN-
CHORAGE FOR VESSELS OF ALL
SHAPES, SIZES, PURPOSES, AND OWN-
ERSHIPS, INCLUDING THOSE OF THE
THRIVING CRUISE LINE INDUSTRY
WHICH SPRANG UP IN THE 1980S.
AFTER THE ALASKAN OIL SPILL IN
1989, THE *EXXON VALDEZ* CALLED
AT SAN DIEGO FOR REPAIRS AT
NASSCO SHIPYARDS AND THEN PUT
OUT TO SEA AGAIN AS THE *EXXON
MEDITERRANEAN.*

SAN DIEGO UNION TRIBUNE / JOHN GIBBINS

SAN DIEGO UNION TRIBUNE / MICHAEL PAUL FRANKLIN

A T THE FOOT OF PRESIDIO HILL SITS OLD TOWN, WHERE THE YOUNG SETTLEMENT OF SAN DIEGO FIRST TOOK ON MUNICIPAL FORM. TODAY THE GLEAMING SKYLINE OF SAN DIEGO'S "NEW" TOWN CONTINUES TO RISE A FEW MILES TO THE SOUTH, WHILE THE SHOPS, RESTAURANTS, AND HISTORIC BUILDINGS OF OLD TOWN PRESERVE AN AMBIANCE IN WHICH SWIRLING, COLORFUL SPANISH FESTIVALS NATURALLY AND REGULARLY OCCUR.

A 20-MINUTE DRIVE BRINGS THE SAN DIEGAN ACROSS THE BORDER INTO MEXICO AND THE BORDER METROPOLIS OF TIJUANA. FROM TIJUANA, A HIGHWAY WINDS SOUTH ALONG SOME OF THE MOST SPECTACULAR COASTLINE IN THE WORLD. VISITORS REGULARLY MAKE THE HOUR-LONG DRIVE TO THE PORT OF ENSENADA FOR SCENERY AND SEAFOOD OR STOP HALFWAY DOWN AT ROSARITO FOR MARGARITAS AND BULLFIGHTS.

O LD TOWN IS THE PLACE WHERE 19TH-CENTURY SAN DIEGANS WORKED AND LIVED AND PLAYED AND WORSHIPPED. WORSHIP HAS CONTINUED VIRTUALLY WITHOUT PAUSE SINCE THE OLD DAYS IN OLD TOWN'S CHURCH OF THE IMMACULATE CONCEPTION, BUT THE CITY'S COMMERCIAL AND RESIDENTIAL ACTIVITY FOUND CENTERS ELSEWHERE. COMMERCIALLY, OLD TOWN IS BUSTLING AGAIN; SEVERAL VICTORIAN HOMES HAVE BEEN MOVED INTO THE AREA AND RESTORED AS HERITAGE PARK.

S TROLLERS CAN FOLLOW A WALKWAY EAST FROM THE
PRADO IN BALBOA PARK PAST THE SHOPS IN SPANISH
VILLAGE TOWARD THE PARKING LOTS AND ENTRANCE TO
THE SAN DIEGO ZOO. EN ROUTE, THEY WILL PASS BY AN
AMUSEMENT AREA WHERE A GASOLINE-POWERED, SCALE-
MODEL RAILROAD TRAIN TAKES CHILDREN AND ADULTS
ALIKE ON A GREEN, PASTORAL LOOP. AND OPPOSITE THE
RAILROAD IS THE EVER-POPULAR BALBOA PARK CAROUSEL.

BENEATH THE EASTERN APPROACH RAMPS TO THE
CORONADO BRIDGE, BOLD COUNTENANCES, IN THE
COLORFUL STYLE OF MEXICAN ARTISTS, HIGHLIGHT
MURALS THAT TRANSFORM SUPPORT PIERS INTO WORKS OF
ART. OPENED IN 1969, THE BRIDGE PASSES DIRECTLY
OVER CHICANO PARK AS IT RISES FROM THE MAINLAND
SIDE ON ITS TWO-MILE REACH TO THE RESIDENCES,
NAVY FACILITIES, AND LANDMARK GRAND HOTEL ON
CORONADO.

E VERY PURSUIT OF A DREAM PASSES
THROUGH UNFULFILLED STAGES.
THE IDEA OF A SCHOOLHOUSE IN
TIJUANA'S EL FLORIDO SECTION
WAS PUT ON HOLD AT THE FRAMING
STAGE WHEN FUNDING RAN OUT.
THE GOALS OF EDUCATION, HOW-
EVER, REMAINED IN SIGHT, AND
CLASSES CONTINUED. IN SAN
DIEGO AT DR. MARTIN LUTHER
KING JR. ELEMENTARY SCHOOL,
STUDENT RACQUEL YARBOROUGH
GIVES DR. KING'S "I HAVE A
DREAM" SPEECH DURING A CELE-
BRATION HONORING THE CIVIL
RIGHTS LEADER'S BIRTHDAY.

SAN DIEGO UNION TRIBUNE / BARRY FITZSIMMONS

JERRY RIFE

A T SCHOOL, CHILDREN PAINT. THEY
GET SOME OF IT ON THE CANVAS,
TOO. THEY PAINT WHAT THEY SEE
IN VIVID IMAGINATIONS AS YET
UNFETTERED BY THE RULES AND
REGULATIONS OF CHEMISTRY, BIOL-
OGY, AND PHYSICS. THERE IS NOTH-
ING IN YOUNG IMAGINATIONS THAT
SAYS ALL THE MOUNTAINS CAN'T BE
ICE CREAM AND THAT THE SUN
CAN'T BE AS WATCHABLE AS THE
MOON, RISING EVERY MORNING
WITH A BIG SMILE.

KUBLA KAHN, CAMELOT, AND OTHER IN-
SPIRED AND STEEPLED CIVILIZATIONS RISE
ANNUALLY IN SAND CASTLE COMPETITIONS
AT SAN DIEGO'S BEACHES, WHERE THE
ARCHITECTS TAKE THEIR WORK SERI-
OUSLY.(PREVIOUS PAGES)
Marti Kranzberg photo

CLIMBING CLUBS MEET REGULARLY TO
SCALE THE ROCK FACES IN UPPER MISSION
GORGE, WHICH PROVIDES EXCELLENT
PRACTICE FOR MORE SHEER CHALLENGES
IN THE INLAND MOUNTAINS AND THE
SIERRA NEVADA. THE SAN DIEGO RIVER
CUT THE GORGE ON ITS ROUTE FROM THE
CUYAMACAS TO MISSION VALLEY. THE
EARTHEN PADRE DAM, BUILT ACROSS THE
RIVER BY SPANISH MISSIONARIES, IS EVI-
DENCE OF THE LONG STRUGGLE TO MAN-
AGE WATER RESOURCES IN AN ARID LAND.

O LD PASTIMES CONTINUALLY DEVELOP NEW WRINKLES IN THE CAPITALS OF SPORT AND RECREATION. SOMEBODY STARTED WONDERING WHAT WOULD HAPPEN IF A SAIL- BOAT WAS CROSSED WITH A SURFBOARD, AND THE SPORT OF WINDSURFING WAS BORN. IT IS A TRICKY BUSINESS AND AN EXHILARATING ONE, ONCE ONE GETS THE HANG OF IT, AS THESE MISSION BAY STUDENTS HOPE TO DO.

S PEAKING OF EXHILARATING, HANG GLIDING IS ABOUT AS
CLOSE AS PEOPLE HAVE COME TO SPROUTING WINGS.
HANG GLIDERS PRACTICE THEIR AIRY GAMES WHEREVER A
DECENT UPDRAFT CAN BE FOUND; THEY ARE SEEN
JUMPING OFF INLAND RIDGE LINES ALL THE TIME. BUT
THE OCEAN WINDS ARRIVING AT THE TORREY PINES
CLIFFS PROVIDE THE BEST AND MOST SCENIC UPDRAFTS OF
ALL.

SAN DIEGO UNION TRIBUNE / CHRIS CAVANAUGH

SAN DIEGO UNION TRIBUNE / RICK McCARTHY

BARRY FITZSIMMONS

O N ANY GIVEN DAY IN SAN DIEGO WATERS, THE PREDOMI-
NANT MOTIVE POWER IS PROVIDED BY SAIL. ON PERIODIC
FESTIVAL DATES WHEN SAILING IS CELEBRATED, MASTERS
OF THE *STAR OF INDIA* TAKE HER FROM HER MARITIME

MUSEUM MOORAGE ON THE EMBARCADERO FOR A TURN
OFF POINT LOMA, WHERE SHE CUTS AS STRIKING A FIGURE
AS SHE DID IN THE 19TH CENTURY. ON OTHER DAYS,
SLEEK CATS CUT LAZY WAKES IN THE SHIMMERING WAVES.

For decades, every evening when the sun settled into the western horizon for the night, it handed off the flame to the old lighthouse high on the Point Loma promontory, where now stands Cabrillo National Monument. During the night, the lighthouse showed seafarers where Point Loma was, then at dawn handed the duty back to the sun. Today a newer lighthouse right on the point handles the chore with its beacon at the top of a stairway that spirals upward like a nautilus chamber.

O F THE UNITED STATES FORCES SENT TO THE PERSIAN GULF DURING THE CONFLICT OF 1990-91, ONE SOLDIER OR SAILOR IN EIGHT WAS SAN DIEGO-BASED. SINCE WORLD WAR I, MEN, WOMEN, AND OCCASIONAL OTHER RECRUITS, HAVE PASSED THROUGH "BOOT CAMP" IN SAN DIEGO ON THEIR WAY TO CONFLICTS AROUND THE GLOBE. EVEN IN PEACETIME TEARFUL FAREWELLS AND JOYFUL REUNIONS COME AND GO WITH THE REGULARITY OF THE SEASONS. AND SOME WARRIORS RETURN TO DWELL, FINALLY, IN THE FIELD OF MARKERS AT FORT ROSECRANS.

A PAIR OF ARCHITECTURAL MARVELS, ONE MORE WHIMSICAL THAN THE OTHER, GRACE THE SAN DIEGO COASTLINE. A MISSION BEACH LANDMARK, THE GIANT DIPPER ROLLER COASTER WAS BUILT IN THE 1920S AND HAS BEEN EMULATING CLOUD FORMATIONS EVER SINCE. A FEW MILES NORTH IN LA JOLLA, DR. JONAS SALK STANDS IN THE COURTYARD OF HIS SALK INSTITUTE, CONSIDERED ONE OF THE WORLD'S ARCHITECTURAL JEWELS.

THE GIANT DIPPER, A UNIQUE
WOODEN ROLLER COASTER, STOOD
IDLE FOR YEARS AND WAS IN DAN-
GER OF DEMOLITION. IN THE
1980S, A CITIZENS' GROUP FORMED
THE "SAVE THE COASTER COMMIT-
TEE" AND WENT TO WORK. RESTO-
RATION WAS SLOW AND DEPEND-
ENT ON UNCERTAIN FUNDING (THE
COMMITTEE HOSTED MORE THAN
ONE CHILI COOK-OFF), BUT BY 1990
THE COASTER WAS AGAIN TAKING
RIDERS FOR SCARY TURNS ABOVE
MISSION BEACH.

"**N**O PAIN, NO GAIN." SO THEY SAY IN THE FITNESS TRADE, WHICH IN SOUTHERN CALIFORNIA IS A PRETTY BIG INDUSTRY. BICYCLISTS BY THE HUNDREDS — MAYBE THOUSANDS — ASSEMBLE FOR THE DUBIOUS PLEASURE OF RACING 60 OR 70 MILES OVER GRUELING BAJA CALIFORNIA ROUTES. AT A MORE ADVANCED LEVEL, WORLD-CLASS CYCLISTS COMPETE ANNUALLY IN THE LA JOLLA GRAND PRIX. BUT SOUTHERN CALIFORNIA'S SIGNATURE FITNESS EVENT IS THE 10-KILOMETER RUN; THIS ONE BENEFITED THE LEUKEMIA SOCIETY.

From the Anza-Borrego desert, this is the same view that greeted early explorers and settlers making their way into Southern California. (Previous Pages) Beyond the mountains lies San Diego, which many bypassed because of the easier route into the Los Angeles Basin.
San Diego Union Tribune / Charlie Neuman photo

The Anza-Borrego Desert State Park is a true low desert (at El Centro, the elevation drops below sea level) that reaches from Riverside County on the north almost to Mexico on the south. Thanks to irrigation from the Colorado River, the area's Imperial Valley is one of the nation's most productive agricultural areas. Beyond the cultivation, however, the flora is strictly adapted to desert rainfall.

THE DESERT MAY SEEM BLEAK, BUT IT HAS ITS CHAMPIONS.
PEOPLE WHO HAVE SEEN THE DESERT AT DAWN AND
TWILIGHT AND AT NIGHT WILL TELL YOU THERE IS NO
BEAUTY MORE BREATHTAKING. AND THERE IS ABUNDANT
DESERT LIFE. MANY SAN DIEGANS MAKE THE ANNUAL
SPRING TREK TO ANZA-BORREGO TO SEE THE BLOOMS
COAXED FROM THE DESERT FLOOR BY THE WINTER RAINS.

I N THE NATIVE AMERICAN PHILOS-
OPHY, ALL THINGS — PEOPLE,
ANIMALS, FLOWERS, MOUNTAINS,
SKY — EXIST IN HARMONY, AND
THE INDIANS' RITUAL IS AN
EXPRESSION OF THAT HARMONY.
THE RITUAL DRESS, INVOKING
THE MYTHOLOGY OF NON-WEST-
ERN ART, APPEARS SIMPLY TO
REPEAT THE COLORS AND THEMES
OF THE EARTH SPIRITS, WHEN IN
FACT THE SPIRIT OF THE FLOWER
IS PRESENT IN THE HEADDRESS.

Tribes from across the United States meet at the Indian Fair in Balboa Park. The late mythologist Joseph Campbell said his fascination with mythology first rose in him when, as a youth, he went to the Buffalo Bill Wild West Show and watched Indians dancing. Author D.H. Lawrence said he first understood religion when he saw the Indian ritual dances in New Mexico.

LOUISE A. PALAZOLA

THE ROLLING HILLS OF COASTAL SOUTHERN CALIFORNIA ARE OFTEN DRAPED WITH SYMMETRIC PATTERNS OF CULTIVATION. CITRUS IS THE REGION'S TRADEMARK CROP, THOUGH A VARIETY OF SAN DIEGO COUNTY PRODUCE, FROM AVOCADOS TO ZUCCHINI, FINDS ITS WAY TO TABLES ACROSS THE NATION. FARMING IS NOT THE AGRICULTURAL FORCE IT ONCE WAS, HOWEVER, BECAUSE OF SUBURBAN SPREAD AND A DROUGHT THAT BEGAN IN THE 1980S.

Tourists passing through North County on Interstate 5 are frequently startled to see sudden
huge blocks of color covering the ground east of
the freeway. These are the flower fields at
Carlsbad which supply flowers to retailers nationwide. Visitors frequent the fields at the height
of the season, their vehicles lining the frontage
road and streets in the area.

W HAT GOES AROUND, COMES AROUND. THE LIGHTS OF THE
CITY'S NIGHT CYCLE APPEAR TO SWIRL BENEATH THE
PLEXIGLAS BUBBLE OF A SLOWLY ROTATING POLICE
HELICOPTER. OVERHEAD, THE EARTH'S CYCLE THROUGH
NIGHT IS RECORDED FROM SAN DIEGO STATE UNIVER-
SITY'S MT. LAGUNA OBSERVATORY BY A PHOTOGRAPHER
WHO ZEROED HIS TIME EXPOSURE ON POLARIS, THE
NORTH STAR.

O N MOST WEEKENDS SAN DIEGO TAKES ON A
DOWNRIGHT CARNIVAL AIR. THE WEATHER
WILL BE PLEASANT 95 PERCENT OF THE
TIME; THE PADRES, SAN DIEGO'S ENTRY IN
THE NATIONAL BASEBALL LEAGUE, GET
RAINED OUT MAYBE ONCE EVERY THREE OR
FOUR YEARS. BALLOONS MAKE COLORFUL
FLIGHTS FROM DEL MAR ACROSS THE
NORTH COUNTY FOOTHILLS. THE BAYS
SPARKLE UNDER SUNLIGHT AND SAIL,
CLOWNS WELCOME SEAPORT VILLAGE VISI-
TORS, AND WARM BREEZES WAFT BUTTER-
FLIES ON THEIR LAZY ROUNDS.

JENNIE REDFIELD

JERRY RIFE

LOUISE A. PALAZZOLA

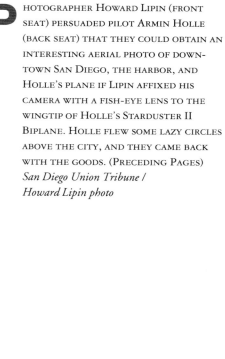

Photographer Howard Lipin (front seat) persuaded pilot Armin Holle (back seat) that they could obtain an interesting aerial photo of downtown San Diego, the harbor, and Holle's plane if Lipin affixed his camera with a fish-eye lens to the wingtip of Holle's Starduster II Biplane. Holle flew some lazy circles above the city, and they came back with the goods. (Preceding Pages)
San Diego Union Tribune / Howard Lipin photo

In a normal year, November marks the beginning of the rainy season, with rainfall—mostly from Pacific storms—on and off through the end of March. Accumulations vary according to topography: if the coast gets an inch, the Cuyamaca and Laguna mountains can expect two or three inches. And if the storm is cold enough, snow will fall in the mountains. Occasionally a weather anomaly will bring a tropical disturbance up from the south, with effects more common to Oklahoma or Texas. But mostly in San Diego, it just rains confetti.

SINCE THE 1960S, SAN DIEGO
HAS BUILT BRIDGES TOWARD
BOTH THE FUTURE AND THE
PAST. THE CORONADO
BRIDGE, FROM DOWNTOWN
ACROSS THE HARBOR TO THE
CITY OF CORONADO, WAS
OPENED IN 1969. IN DOWN-
TOWN SAN DIEGO THERE
CONTINUES THE RESTORATION
CONTINUES ON THE TURN-OF-
THE-20TH-CENTURY BUILD-
INGS IN THE GASLAMP
QUARTER, A DISTRICT OF
HOTELS, SHOPS, AND
RESTAURANTS.

JERRY RIFE

IN THE BACKGROUND,
SAN DIEGO'S GLASS AND STEEL
SAILS OF COMMERCE RISE TO
CATCH THE WINDS OF THE
21ST CENTURY. (PRECEDING
PAGES) IN THE FOREGROUND,
THE MASTS OF SAN DIEGO'S
RECREATIONAL SKYLINE
STAND AT REST FOR THE
MOMENT AT THE SAN DIEGO
YACHT CLUB.
Don Kohlbauer photo

MARTI KRANZBERG

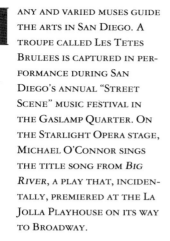

MANY AND VARIED MUSES GUIDE
THE ARTS IN SAN DIEGO. A
TROUPE CALLED LES TETES
BRULEES IS CAPTURED IN PER-
FORMANCE DURING SAN
DIEGO'S ANNUAL "STREET
SCENE" MUSIC FESTIVAL IN
THE GASLAMP QUARTER. ON
THE STARLIGHT OPERA STAGE,
MICHAEL O'CONNOR SINGS
THE TITLE SONG FROM BIG
RIVER, A PLAY THAT, INCIDEN-
TALLY, PREMIERED AT THE LA
JOLLA PLAYHOUSE ON ITS WAY
TO BROADWAY.

THE RELATIONSHIP OF THE PHYSICAL AND SPIRITUAL FINDS MANY EXPRESSIONS IN THE SOUTHERN CALIFORNIA AND SAN DIEGO LIFESTYLE, A LIFESTYLE THAT INSPIRES GENTLE SATIRE IN MORE CONVENTIONAL PARTS OF THE NATION. VEGETARIANS USUALLY TAKE THE RIBBING IN GOOD HUMOR AND IN THEIR RESTAURANTS GO ABOUT THE BUSINESS OF EXPERIMENTING WITH MEATLESS VARIATIONS OF EVERYTHING FROM HAMBURGERS TO CHILI.

Ⓞ N THE OTHER HAND, HUNGRY PEO-
PLE WILL FIND WHATEVER THEIR
TASTE BUDS DESIRE AMONG SAN
DIEGO'S HUNDREDS OF EATERIES,
FROM HAUTE CUISINE TO ICE CREAM
SUNDAES. AT THE CORVETTE DINER
IN HILLCREST WAITRESSES LIKE JILL
DILLENDER SERVE UP CONFECTIONS
THAT SEEM STRAIGHT FROM THE
'50S. IN LITTLE ITALY ALONG INDIA
STREET THE SCENTS OF GARLIC,
BASIL, OREGANO, AND TOMATOES
SWIRL FROM CAFES INTO THE STREET.

ON JANUARY 5, 1992, WITH HUN-
DREDS OF THOUSANDS OF PEOPLE
WATCHING, THE SETTING SUN
NEARED THE WESTERN HORIZON
AND STARTED TO CATCH UP WITH
THE MOON. ALMOST AT THE MO-
MENT OF SUNSET, THE MOON BE-
CAME CENTERED IN THE SUN'S
FACE, AN EVENT CALLED AN "ANNU-
LAR ECLIPSE" WHICH WON'T OCCUR
AGAIN FOR 20,000 YEARS. THE
ECLIPSE IN TOTAL ANNULARITY
COULD BE SEEN FOR HUNDREDS OF
MILES ALONG THE PACIFIC COAST,
BUT ITS CENTER—THE AXIS OF THE
SUN THROUGH THE MOON—WAS
ENCINITAS, A SAN DIEGO COASTAL
SUBURB.

THE FUTURE BECKONS

I N A LARGER ODYSSEY—IN SAN DIEGO'S OWN PASSAGE, AS A CITY AND A METROPOLITAN AREA, TOWARD THE 21ST CENTURY—THESE ARE EXCITING TIMES. NO ONE COULD IDENTIFY THE EXACT MOMENT THAT IT HAPPENED, BUT SAN DIEGO, AFTER A LONG ADOLESCENCE, HAS SUDDENLY EMERGED AS A CIVIC CINDERELLA, READY TO TAKE HER TURN ON THE INTERNATIONAL BALLROOM FLOOR. ◆ INTERESTINGLY, THIS HAPPENS AT A TIME WHEN CALIFORNIA THREATENS TO TURN INTO A PUMPKIN. *TIME* MAGAZINE, IN THE FALL OF 1991, PUBLISHED A SPECIAL ISSUE TITLED "CALIFORNIA: THE ENDANGERED DREAM" ABOUT THE STATE'S PROBLEMS WITH POPULATION, POLLUTION, AND BUSINESS CLIMATE. ON THE COVER OF THAT ISSUE WAS A PHOTO OF THE SUN, OSTENSIBLY SETTING OVER WHAT WAS ONCE THE GOLDEN LAND. IN SAN DIEGO, THE REACTION WAS AS IF CINDERELLA HAD ARRIVED JUST AS THE BAND WAS PACKING UP TO GO HOME. EVERYONE DOWN HERE WAS SAYING, "WAIT A MINUTE..." ◆ SO SAN DIEGO'S CHALLENGE IN THE 20TH CENTURY'S LAST DECADE IS A CURIOUS, SEEMINGLY CONTRADICTORY ONE. THE CITY WILL HAVE TO MANAGE SUCCESS AND EGRESS AT THE SAME TIME. AS IT PERFORMS THE DUTIES OF CHARMING HOSTESS, IT WILL HAVE TO DEAL WITH ITS OWN UGLY STEP-SISTERS OF GROWTH—CONGESTION, CRIME, INADEQUATE FACILITIES, OVERBURDENED RE-SOURCES—AS IT DEALS WITH THE RECESSIVE EFFECTS OF BUSINESSES FLEEING THE STATE'S STORMY BUSINESS CLIMATE—ONE IN FOUR, BY A LATE 1991 POLL. ◆ THE STATE'S PROBLEMS, HOWEVER, ARE NOT GOING TO SCUTTLE THE CITY'S HOUR OF SUCCESS. TOO MUCH MOMENTUM IS AT WORK, FOUR-AND-A-HALF CENTURIES OF IT, WITH ELEMENTS QUIETLY FALLING INTO PLACE A GENERATION AT A TIME. THE LAST ELEMENT, WATER, ARRIVED FROM THE COLORADO RIVER IN 1947. WATER WAS CINDERELLA'S GLASS SLIPPER. WITH IT, EVERYTHING ABOUT SAN DIEGO STARTED TO FIT. BY 1960, THE REGION'S POPULATION NEARLY DOUBLED TO 1.03 MILLION, AND SAN DIEGO WAS ON ITS WAY. THE CITY NOW SEEMS TO HAVE TAKEN ON A LIFE AND A DIRECTION OF ITS OWN. IT IS AS IF

*Visitors to Horton Plaza, the centerpiece of downtown revitaliza-tion, quickly find that it is not just another shopping mall.
(Jennie Redfield photo)*

success stole up on San Diego while no one, not even in San Diego, was looking.

Civic critics in the 1970s and '80s made a career of deploring the city's "lack of leadership." If that is so, then gremlins and godmothers must have brought the city to the threshold where she stands today. The Gaslamp Quarter redevelopment downtown, starting at Broadway and pointing like an arrow to the new harborside Convention Center, must have happened by some midnight spontaneity. The Convention Center must have sprung up from some magic bean dropped fortuitously at that exact spot. Pacific Rim movers and shakers arriving in San Diego for 1992 meetings must have been guided by a star in the East. San Diego's bitter, successful fight against Southern California Edison's attempted take-over of the hometown power company must have been managed by aliens from outer space. The Super Bowl in 1988, the America's Cup and the Major League All-Star Game in 1992, the Tony award in 1984 to the Globe for regional theater, the establishment of world research centers, the Tomahawk missile, the Pulitzer Prizes, the Nobel laureates, Dr. Seuss (Ted Geisel, who spun his magic from a seaside La Jolla studio), all must have flown off the tip of a magic wand.

So it seems. Probably no city on the continent has a more romantic history, but the fairy tale quality of San Diego's progress really started to get serious around 1972. The city already was a promising neophyte in national sports circles with the Chargers and the Padres. San Diego's

name was known to scientists and academicians worldwide because the Atlas Centaur rocket, today a mainstay in NASA's growing space program, was built here. The city had even suffered a major-league disaster with the failure in the commercial airlines marketplace of the locally built Convair 880 and 990 jetliners.

Then the Republican National Committee named San Diego the site of the GOP's 1972 presidential nominating convention, to be held at the new Sports Arena. But the GOP started fussing about hotel rooms and eventually reneged and moved the '72 convention to Miami Beach. San Diego blushed deeply, but when the August week arrived for the convention that would have been, then-mayor Pete Wilson dabbed on a bit of civic Clearasil and proclaimed it "America's Finest City Week."

Thus did the adolescent Cinderella begin to stir. Looking in the mirror, she saw that the natural beauty there had begun to mature. It was an interesting moment. For more than 100 years San Diego had yearned for the national stature that had been channeled by quirks of geography to Los Angeles. Now the day of that stature was dawning and with it came a sense of inevitability. Like it or not, San Diego was going to join an exalted community of cities. There was no longer a choice. She was pretty, and now she had to be good.

It wouldn't be easy. Troubled guardians sounded warnings all along about an inevitable collision with reality. By the end of the 1980s, the regional population was around 2.5 million. The beauty in the mirror then was stunning but

TOO MUCH MOMENTUM IS AT WORK, FOUR AND A HALF CENTURIES OF IT, WITH ELEMENTS QUIETLY FALLING INTO PLACE A GENERATION AT A TIME. THE LAST ELEMENT, WATER, ARRIVED FROM THE COLORADO RIVER IN 1947. WATER WAS CINDERELLA'S GLASS SLIPPER. WITH IT, EVERYTHING ABOUT SAN DIEGO STARTED TO FIT.

having difficulty slipping into a size eight. The guardians had said it would come to this one day, that the once lovely city, the "sleepy Navy town," would be wallowing in size sixteens, just like Los Angeles.

Poor Los Angeles. It gets such a terrible rap, when in fact Los Angeles proper is a lovely city with wide streets, a healthy mix of cultures, and a handsome, vibrant downtown district that ranks as a world-class cultural center. The trouble with Los Angeles is not Los Angeles. The trouble is the automobile.

Was San Diego steering for the same trouble? In 1987, during "America's Finest City Week," a local newspaper conducted a poll: Should San Diego still call itself "America's Finest City," or, if not, then what? The poll ran 5-to-1 against "AFC" and sparked some fine satire. Among the replacement suggestions: "San Diego—Formerly America's Finest City"; "City of $200,000 Condos"; "City of Baja Los Angeles"; "Where the Turf Meets the Sewage"; and "Occasional Home of America's Cup."

On the flip side, a few respondents rejected "America's Finest City" because they thought it no longer said enough about San Diego. A suggested replacement: "Rainbow's End." It has not been adopted, but its fairy-tale quality reflects the city's recent experience.

The question is how to live happily ever after. All the discussions about San Diego's future spin around two propositions, one real and the other negotiable. Growth is the real proposition, and the negotiable one is quality. In the old days, as with love and marriage, there could not be one without the other. These days, however, it is

common to have love without marriage, though it strains morality. So it goes with growth and quality. Some say San Diego's recent growth strains morality; if the growth-quality proprieties are not restored, the rainbow's end will become only a tantalizing vision, visible but inaccessible.

In 1991, a citizens' group called "PLAN!" (Prevent Los Angelization Now!) published a San Diego growth theory that saw population "waves" spreading like concrete tsunamis across Southern California from the Los Angeles epicenter. The first wave, in the 1800s, populated Los Angeles itself. The second wave, 100 years later, rolled south into Orange County pushed by economic and political forces. About 1980 when Orange County had been "built out," a third wave rolled inland inundating Riverside and San Bernardino counties. That process, suggested PLAN!, is still under way. When it is completed, a fourth wave will roll south—toward, and then over, San Diego.

"With this fourth growth wave," said PLAN!, "will come the more than 1 million additional people expected to flood into San Diego County by the year 2005. The end result will be freeway gridlock, severe mandatory water conservation measures, more than a hundred days of polluted air, the collapse of our school system, gang warfare, a mushrooming crime rate, chronic overcrowding of parks and libraries, and a crushing tax and fee burden."

Preventing such horrors, suggested PLAN!, was possible if regional governments and planners put into motion planning solutions that had been "well-known since the early 1970s."

Within days of the report's publication a

> **B**Y THE END OF THE 1980S, THE REGIONAL POPULATION WAS AROUND 2.5 MILLION. THE BEAUTY IN THE MIRROR THEN WAS STUNNING, BUT WAS HAVING DIFFICULTY SLIPPING INTO A SIZE EIGHT.

coalition of San Diegans, including a former congressman and the Chamber of Commerce president, published an analysis taking strong exception to the PLAN! scenario. This opposing piece pointed to strong control factors already in place including "protection of favorable topographical conditions, stringent environmental regulations that preclude development on much of our remaining undeveloped land, and the expansion of mass transit." The analysis further stated, "These factors and slower economic activity indicate that tomorrow's growth will occur along established transit corridors, reinvigorating older communities in ways less dependent on the automobile." Examples of control factors already in place but developing continuously are two regional parks, the Mission Trails and San Dieguito parks, which follow river courses from the foothills across the coastal plain to the sea.

When people speak of San Diego in terms of planning and population and the future, they are talking about a region generally defined by San Diego County that abuts Orange and Riverside counties on the north, reaches east to the edge of the Imperial Valley, and has its south boundary on the international border with Mexico. Within this region are 19 government jurisdictions—18 cities and the county itself. These jurisdictions are associated through a regional planning agency called the San Diego Association of Governments (SANDAG). During the 1980s San Diego's population grew phenomenally, at a rate of 3 percent annually. SANDAG in 1991 released a regional study showing that although San Diego's population will increase from less than 2.5 million to almost 4 million by the year 2015, the region's growth rate will slow to an average of 1.9 percent annually.

Any discussion of planning in the San Diego area must also include Tijuana, the sprawling Mexican border metropolis whose affairs will forever be intertwined with those of San Diego. Although the two areas have contrasting cultures and qualities of life, a vision is developing in both communities of a future whose brightness can only be guaranteed by transcending boundaries. Tijuana's emergence as a manufacturing center, for example, has import for the entire region.

SANDAG's new population forecast was a revision of one released in 1988 and shows the vagaries of the planning business. Growth estimates in 1991 were higher than in 1988 because of an escalation in the regional birth rate, among other things. San Diego, a military town, experienced a baby boom after the Persian Gulf "Desert Storm" action of 1990-91. The new San Diego Naval Hospital, which serves more than 400,000 active and retired military personnel and their families, predicted a 10 percent increase in births in December and January of 1991-92 after the passion of the soldiers' return the previous March and April.

Whatever its glitches, the planning activity is well developed in San Diego; it experiences frequent noisy bursts, which is a good sign. There has also developed within the civic planning process, with its built-in boosterism, a streak of realism provoked by a desire to get results. The Centre City Development Corporation, a city agency, has become both defender and critic of the downtown districts it seeks to revitalize.

THE QUESTION IS, HOW TO LIVE HAPPILY EVER AFTER. ALL THE DISCUSSIONS ABOUT SAN DIEGO'S FUTURE SPIN AROUND TWO PROPOSITIONS, ONE REAL AND THE OTHER NEGOTIABLE. GROWTH IS THE REAL PROPOSITION, AND THE NEGOTIABLE ONE IS QUALITY.

Despite the completion of a 15-year plan that brought $1.4 billion in private investment to downtown and changed the shape of the city's skyline, a new report prepared by CCDC in 1991 acknowledged worsening downtown decay, crime, and blight. It was a frankness required to justify the need for continued special redevelopment powers available through state government. If approved by the City Council, the plan, which envisions $1.9 billion in tax supports, would stimulate more than $22 billion in private investment downtown over the next 35 years.

Much of the need for downtown redevelopment, as in any large American city, arises from fair wear and tear. The cities that first rose in the late 1800s and early 1900s are now, simply put, old. What doesn't deserve restoring needs replacing. San Diego's downtown, at this point in the process, is an exciting mix of both—the Gaslamp Quarter representing restoration at its most detailed, and the towers along B Street and lower Broadway representing visions of tomorrow. The San Diego difference, however, is that its downtown plan is not only an obligation of renewal but a passage of emergence. In the world's eyes, San Diego is the new belle of the ball with suitors lining up for a space on her dance card.

On February 26, 1983, the British royal yacht *Britannia* entered Diego Bay and tied up at Broadway Pier. In the fullness of time as prescribed by protocol, Queen Elizabeth II of England debarked the ship, becoming the first reigning British monarch to visit the United States' West Coast. Residents will remember for a long time how beautiful the city was for the occasion. San Diego, the eager young American princess, made her best curtsy and showed Her Majesty a royal time in cool, rainy February weather. The Queen and Prince Philip visited the aircraft carrier *Ranger*, the Old Globe Theater, the Museum of Art, the Scripps Institution of Oceanography, and Saint Paul's Episcopal Church. Wherever she went, cheering San Diegans lined the avenues. A memorable event occurred when San Diego's deputy mayor, in an endearing slip of provincialism, touched Her Majesty on the back as he guided her off a dais. It made international headlines.

More international headlines followed when the America's Cup, symbol of world yacht-racing supremacy, found a new home at the San Diego Yacht Club after skipper Dennis Conner's *Stars and Stripes* defeated the Australian boat, four races to none, off Fremantle, Australia early in 1987. Even bigger headlines came the following year after an extraordinary Cup challenge which was decided in San Diego waters but was finally resolved on drawing boards and in courtrooms. (After the spray had settled, a *New Yorker* magazine analysis suggested the boats should have been named *Plaintiff* and *Defendant*.)

The 1988 challenger from New Zealand took advantage of a loophole in the 150-year-old America's Cup bylaws to build a beautiful boat that was a radical departure from the traditional 12-meter America's Cup design—and also much faster. If they can do it, said Conner, so can we. The Conner team designed and built a catamaran with a "sail" designed on the principles of an airplane's wing and made of space-age materials. Consultants on the catamaran were designers of

ANY DISCUSSION OF PLANNING IN THE SAN DIEGO AREA MUST ALSO INCLUDE TIJUANA, THE SPRAWLING MEXICAN BORDER METROPOLIS WHOSE AFFAIRS WILL FOREVER BE INTERTWINED WITH THOSE OF SAN DIEGO.

the *Voyager*, the first aircraft to fly non-stop around the world without refueling (in 1986). Conner's boat swept the series, winning the last race by more than 21 minutes. New Zealand sued, claiming the American multi-hull design was illegal. After a series of verdicts and appeals in the New York Supreme Court, the Cup remained in San Diego, where challengers from around the world arrived in 1991 to prepare for the '92 regatta.

In 1989 at San Diego's invitation, a contingent of Russian, Georgian and other artists, performers, and entertainers, and a display of rare, jewel-encrusted Faberge eggs arrived for a week-long Soviet Arts Festival, the first event of its kind in the *glasnost* era.

Later that same year San Diego's new $165 million Convention Center, with its distinctive architecture and sail-like roof, opened on Harbor Drive. The center was expected to emerge as the keystone building in the city's future. In a newspaper think piece, a city councilman saw the new building becoming San Diego's "front porch" on the harbor, a porch facing west on the huge economic potential of the Pacific Rim. The building's managers described a dual role—a hometown hub of local social and business activity and a magnet for future international trade and commerce.

The prospects of that trade and San Diego's steady emergence as an international presence in the 1980s, put pressure on a nagging need the city had talked about for 40 years: a new airport

to replace Lindbergh Field. One intriguing proposal, and one that built a following in the months after its introduction, provided for not one airport, but two: a new airport on the U.S. side straddling the Mexican border and a renovation of Tijuana's existing air terminal on the Mexican side. This "TwinPorts" concept also gave tacit approval to a larger idea, that a merger of San Diego and Tijuana management, trade, and manufacturing resources might eventually transform the region, with its natural, sheltered harbor, into a Pacific Rim business and cultural capital on the order of Hong Kong.

IN A NEWS-PAPER THINK PIECE, A CITY COUNCILMAN SAW THE NEW $165 MILLION CONVENTION CENTER BECOMING SAN DIEGO'S "FRONT PORCH" ON THE HARBOR, A PORCH FACING WEST ON THE HUGE ECONOMIC POTENTIAL OF THE PACIFIC RIM.

That is a vision that might have looked a long way from the troubled, pumpkin-haunted 1990s. But beginning in August of 1990, there began a series of events that reminded Americans—and San Diegans, in particular—of their ability to achieve. On August 2, the nation of Iraq invaded the nation of Kuwait. Within hours of the invasion, two American aircraft carriers, one of them the San Diego-based *Independence*, were diverted to the Persian Gulf. San Diego, a military town, came alert. Any San Diegan, military or civilian, who watched these early developments would have expected events in the Persian Gulf to affect this city.

In the fall, American response to the invasion evolved into Operation Desert Shield. On December 1, an amphibious assault group led by the *Tarawa*, with 13,000 marines and sailors on board, steamed out of San Diego Bay headed for the Persian Gulf. On December 8, the aircraft carrier *Ranger*, with its battle group, followed. On the *Ranger* and the *Independence* and the other U.S. carriers were pilots trained at the Top Gun school at Miramar Naval Air Station in San Diego. In all, 25 San Diego-based Navy ships were sent to the Gulf. By January, with the complete American battle force in place in the Gulf, about 56,000 people—or one in eight service personnel in that force—were from San Diego.

Another associated buildup had been under way in San Diego. The city's industrial community provided war materials: avionics, electronics, parts and equipment, but most spectacularly the Tomahawk missile, manufactured at the General Dynamics plant on Kearny Mesa. Area newspapers and television and radio stations sent crews to the Persian Gulf who filed stories daily about San Diego units and squadrons and their preparations for battle.

At 4 p.m., January 16, San Diego time—early morning of the 17th in the Persian Gulf—U.S. Forces began air and missile attacks on Iraqi positions, and Operation Desert Shield became Desert Storm. *San Diego Union* photographer John R. McCutchen was standing on the deck of the battleship *Wisconsin* as the attack began. His dramatic photo of a Tomahawk missile launch from the *Wisconsin* became the signature image of the world's first truly high tech war.

Back in San Diego there was cheering among General Dynamics designers, engineers, and assemblers as they watched televised reports of the Tomahawk's uncanny accuracy. Americans everywhere watched, amazed, at the images of precision, computerized air warfare.

Whatever the debates over motives and principles, one feature of the conflict stood above comment, and that was achievement. The U.S. international crisis response system not only worked, it worked astonishingly well. That fact alone was a national tonic. Its lasting effect is to remind private and government organizations at all levels that with good planning, good equipment, and good execution, fabulous results are attainable.

It was a positive experience for San Diego to be so directly involved in Desert Storm's successes. The lessons of preparedness cannot help but guide this city as it constructs its view of the future—a future that has high hopes for a fairy-tale ending. The view of that future is to the west, toward the Pacific Rim, and its hub is the new Convention Center. A happy by-product of good planning is the unexpected bonus. Convention Center designers may not have realized that their building would provide a view of the entire San Diego experience. From the rooftop pavilion under the white sails, a person looking west, toward the future, will see the harbor, and the Navy carriers moored at North Island, and then the tip of Point Loma, where stands the statue of Juan Rodriguez Cabrillo.

> IT WAS A POSITIVE EXPERIENCE FOR SAN DIEGO TO BE SO DIRECTLY INVOLVED IN DESERT STORM'S SUCCESSES. THE LESSONS OF PREPAREDNESS CANNOT HELP BUT GUIDE THIS CITY AS IT CONSTRUCTS ITS VIEW OF THE FUTURE—A FUTURE THAT HAS HIGH HOPES FOR A FAIRY-TALE ENDING.

SAN DIEGAN CAROLYN REINERS WATCHED THE JANUARY 5, 1992 ANNULAR ECLIPSE THROUGH SPECIALLY FILTERED BINOCULARS.

S AN DIEGAN CAROLYN REINERS
WATCHED THE JANUARY 5, 1992
ANNULAR ECLIPSE THROUGH
SPECIALLY FILTERED BINOCULARS.
(PREVIOUS PAGES)
*San Diego Union Tribune /
John Nelson photo*

S AN DIEGO'S PREPARATIONS FOR ITS NEXT GENERATION INCLUDE STATE-OF-THE-FUTURE FACILITIES IN BUSINESS, HOTELS, RETAILING, AND TRANSPORTATION. THE DISTINCTIVE NEW CONVENTION CENTER, OVERLOOKING THE HARBOR, ESTABLISHED AN INTERNATIONAL REPUTATION IN ITS FIRST TWO YEARS OF OPERATIONS. THE RED CARS OF THE SAN DIEGO TROLLEY NOW LINK DOWNTOWN WITH THE SOUTH AND EAST SUBURBS, WITH NORTHERN LINKS IN THE WORKS. HORTON PLAZA IS THE ANCHOR OF A MERCHANDISING EFFORT TO ATTRACT SHOPPERS TO DOWNTOWN, AND NEW HOTELS, SUCH AS THE HYATT REGENCY IN THE AVENTINE COMPLEX NORTH OF DOWNTOWN, PROVIDE VISITORS TO THE CITY LUXURIOUS, CONVENIENT ACCOMMODATIONS.

A ND THEY'RRRRRRE OFF! THE
THOROUGHBRED RACING SEASON
AT DEL MAR, THE SEASIDE RACE-
TRACK BUILT BY CROONER BING
CROSBY AND HIS ASSOCIATES IN
THE 1930S, DRAWS HUNDREDS OF
THOUSANDS OF FANS DURING THE
JULY TO SEPTEMBER RACING
SEASON. AFTER THE 1991 SEASON,
TRACK MANAGEMENT RAZED AND
REBUILT THE MAIN GRANDSTAND,
AND THE TRACK OPENED A SATEL-
LITE WAGERING FACILITY THE
SAME YEAR.

THE PADRES (BIP ROBERTS SCORING
HERE) PLAY AN 82-GAME HOME
SCHEDULE AT SAN DIEGO JACK
MURPHY STADIUM. IN THE EARLY
1970S, IT LOOKED LIKE THE TEAM
MIGHT MOVE TO WASHINGTON,
D.C., UNTIL RAY KROC STEPPED UP
AND SAVED THE FRANCHISE BY PUR-
CHASING IT. KROC AND THE CITY
WERE REWARDED FOR THEIR LOY-
ALTY IN 1984, WHEN THE PADRES,
WITH STEVE GARVEY STARRING, WON
THE NATIONAL LEAGUE PENNANT
AND MET DETROIT IN THE WORLD
SERIES.

THE OLYMPICS' EQUESTRIAN EVENTS PICTURED HERE WERE HELD AT FAIRBANKS RANCH IN 1984, AND WORLD-CLASS JUMPING COMPETITION RETURNED TO SAN DIEGO IN 1992 WITH THE VOLVO WORLD CUP AT DEL MAR FAIRGROUNDS. YOUTH SOCCER IS THE MOST POPULAR SPORT IN THE COUNTY, AND THE PROFESSIONAL SAN DIEGO SOCKERS, PLAYING AT THE SPORTS ARENA, HAVE BEEN PERENNIAL CHAMPIONS OF THE NATIONAL INDOOR SOCCER LEAGUES.

S INCE THE LATE 1980S, THE CHARGERS HAVE HAD A HARD TIME LIVING UP TO FANS' EXPECTATIONS AFTER YEARS OF THE 'AIR CORYELL' CHARGERS. THE TEAMS OF THE LATE '70S AND EARLY '80S WON REPEATED DIVISIONAL CHAMPI-ONSHIPS WITH A DAZZLING AERIAL OFFENSE DEVISED BY COACH DON CORYELL AND EXECUTED BY QUARTER-BACK DAN FOUTS. IN THE 1980S, SAN DIEGO JACK MURPHY STADIUM WAS ENLARGED TO ACCOMMODATE THE 1988 SUPER BOWL.

A SCULPTURED INDIAN ON A WOODED PRESIDIO PARK HILLSIDE KEEPS WATCH ON FREEWAY TRAFFIC BELOW (FOLLOWING PAGES). *Jerry Rife photo*

B LIMPS FROM ONE COMPANY OR ANOTHER (THIS ONE FROM GOODYEAR) REGULARLY LEND AERIAL INTEREST TO EVENTS HAPPENING IN THE CITY, INCLUDING THE AMERICA'S CUP WORLD REGATTA IN 1992. SAN DIEGO IS CONTINUALLY FAVORED WITH MAJOR EVENTS IN SPORTS, CULTURE, AND THE ARTS, AS IS BORDER CITY TIJUANA, WHOSE NEW CIVIC FACILITIES INCLUDE THE ROUND OMNIMAX THEATER AT THE CULTURAL CENTER.

THE AREA'S MILITARY SIGNIFICANCE IS NEVER LOST ON RESIDENTS, WHO REGULARLY SEE NAVAL MIGHT AT PRACTICE. SOMETIMES THE MILITARY PUTS ON A SHOW, AS WHEN THE SOVIET NAVY VISITED IN 1990. BUT IN 1991, WHEN EVENTS TURNED SERIOUS, SAN DIEGO'S GENERAL DYNAMICS PROVIDED THE TOMAHAWK MISSILE, HERE BEING LAUNCHED FROM THE BATTLESHIP *WISCONSIN* TOWARD IRAQI FORCES DURING THE PERSIAN GULF WAR.

AFTER A CURIOUS AND CONTROVERSIAL AMERICA'S CUP CHALLENGE BETWEEN NEW ZEALAND AND THE U.S. IN 1988, THE EVENT RETURNS TO SAN DIEGO WATERS IN 1992. YACHTS WERE COMING AND GOING IN THE HARBOR IN EARLY '92 ON PRACTICE RUNS AND PRELIMINARY CHALLENGES, BUILDING TOWARD THE MAY CHAMPION-SHIP. THE SPINNAKERS BELONG TO THE COMPETITORS FROM ITALY AND NEW ZEALAND.

THE SAN DIEGO AREA, INCLUDING ITS BEAUTIFUL HARBOR, IS TOLERANT OF MANY LIFESTYLES AND VARIOUS PURSUITS. SAILBOATS AT REST BELIE THE USUAL LEVEL OF COMMERCIAL WATERFRONT ACTIVITY AND SEEM TO SAY THAT THERE'S ROOM FOR ALL KINDS OF DREAMERS HERE.

SAN DIEGO UNION TRIBUNE / J. T. MacMILLAN

WITH ITS BILLOWING, SAIL-LIKE ROOF, THE SAN DIEGO CONVENTION CENTER IS A STUNNING HARBORSIDE ARCHITECTURAL LANDMARK WHICH ACCOMMODATES THE NEEDS OF LOCAL BUSINESS ACTIVITY AND THE BURGEONING TOURIST INDUSTRY, AS WELL AS STIMULATES INTEREST IN INTERNATIONAL COMMERCE.

PROFILES IN EXCELLENCE

THE SANTA FE RAILWAY STATION WAS BUILT IN SAN DIEGO IN 1887 AS A SPUR OF THE RAIL LINE INTO LOS ANGELES. TODAY IT STILL FUNCTIONS AS THE SOUTH-WEST TERMINUS FOR AMTRAK.

1 8 6 8 - 1 8 9 9

1868

COPLEY NEWSPAPERS

1870

GREATER SAN DIEGO CHAMBER OF COMMERCE

1881

AT&T

1881

SAN DIEGO GAS & ELECTRIC CO.

1887

CITY OF CHULA VISTA

1888

CITY OF CORONADO

1889

SAN DIEGO TRUST & SAVINGS BANK

1890

MERCY HOSPITAL AND MEDICAL CENTER

OR 124 YEARS, THE *San Diego Union-Tribune* newspaper has fulfilled the vision of founder W. Jeff Gatewood: to hold a mirror to the community, allowing the public to see the good and bad, and to provide a point of view on contemporary social and political issues.

POST-CIVIL WAR BEGINNINGS

The Civil War ended just a few years before the paper published its first issue on October 10, 1869. Though California had been a state only a few years, San Diego was already experiencing an influx of newcomers, a westward movement that continues today.

The tiny paper served a dusty village of approximately 3,000 Yankee adventurers, Spanish explorers, missionaries, native American Indians, and Mexicans. But its publisher was a visionary who foresaw a much larger audience, a vast community with "a bay busy with commerce, mammoth mercantile houses, princely residences, and streets teeming with prosperous and industrial people."

Though the newspaper ultimately helped bring about the very things Gatewood had envisioned, it is unlikely that the Civil War-era newspaperman ever thought his paper would one day meet the information needs of several million people in America's sixth largest city. Gatewood, who moved to San Diego from the gold mining town of San Andreas, was certainly a visionary, but he was also a realist. In his first edition, he said the paper "will not have any whisperings of fancy." According to Gatewood, it would be "a faithful mirror...a future reliable historian...and open the way for the march of civilization...inculcate pure morals...lighten tax burdens."

LONGTIME COPLEY LEADERSHIP

After a succession of owners, the original *San Diego Union* newspaper was purchased in 1890 by John D. and Adolph Spreckels, brothers who were local merchants and sugar brokers. The rival *Evening Tribune*, published since December 2, 1895, remained a competitor until it was also bought by the Spreckels brothers in 1901.

TODAY, COPLEY NEWSPAPERS IS A PUBLISHING EMPIRE THAT INCLUDES 11 DAILY NEWSPAPERS, 30 WEEKLIES, AND A HOST OF NEIGHBORHOOD SHOPPERS IN CALIFORNIA AND ILLINOIS. THE COPLEY NEWS SERVICE, WITH ITS EXTENSIVE NETWORK OF CORRESPONDENTS, PROVIDES NEWS AND FEATURES TO 2,000 NEWSPAPER, RADIO, AND TELEVISION CLIENTS AROUND THE WORLD.

In 1928, Colonel Ira Copley from Illinois purchased both the *Union* and the *Tribune*. For several decades, the newspapers operated independently as the city's morning and evening editions, respectively. In 1939, the *Tribune* bought the competing *San Diego Sun* and, in 1950, acquired another rival, the *Daily Journal*. On June 4, 1950, Colonel Copley's son, James S. Copley, became publisher of the *Union* and the *Tribune*. He later moved the Copley Newspapers headquarters from Aurora, Illinois to La Jolla, California.

After James Copley's death in October 1973, his wife Helen K. Copley took a strong leadership role in the parent company, Copley Press, Inc. Continuing the Copley family tradition, she is still publisher, chairman of the board, and chief executive officer, while her son, David Copley, serves as president.

Under the family's longtime leadership, the *Union-Tribune* has been all of the things its founder imagined. Serving the southwestern corner of the United States, the paper maintains a circulation of approximately 400,000 throughout San Diego and Imperial counties. Today, the paper is the flagship of a publishing empire that includes 11 daily newspapers, 30 weeklies, and a host of neighborhood shoppers in California and Illinois. The widely-respected Copley News

The San Diego Union-Tribune, *headquartered today in this building, has served local citizens for 124 years.*

Serving the southwestern corner of the United States, the Union-Tribune *maintains a circulation of approximately 400,000 throughout San Diego and Imperial counties.*

Service, with its extensive network of correspondents, provides news and features to 2,000 newspaper, radio, and television clients around the world. Established in 1955, it has correspondents scattered about the globe and maintains bureaus in Washington, Chicago, Sacramento, Mexico City, Los Angeles, and Springfield.

In 1992, the smaller but spirited and independent *Evening Tribune,* winner of two Pulitzer Prizes, was merged with the stronger Copley flagship newspaper, *The San Diego Union.* The new newspaper concentrates on morning delivery, although it continues to publish two full afternoon editions for home and single copy sales. The staffs and senior editors from the two papers were also integrated. On February 2, 1992, the enlarged newspaper, *The San Diego Union-Tribune,* began a new cycle of newspaper publication featuring the depth of the *Union* and the spice of the *Tribune.* New and greater growth was predicted for what was described as the newspaper of the '90s.

SUPPORTING ALL FACETS OF THE COMMUNITY

Over the years, the Copley family has upheld the *Union-Tribune*'s long tradition as an advocate of citywide improvements and a supporter of community activities. The newspaper's considerable influence brought a railroad and the first highways to San Diego, helping create an economic climate and infrastructure improvements that have attracted major manufacturers. The paper encouraged the creation of the aerospace industry and the conversion of the mud flats of False Bay into Mission Bay Aquatic Park. It has also supported successful efforts to bring a major campus of the University of California to San Diego, establish the research-oriented biological and medical technology industry, build a major sports stadium and world-class convention center, and rejuvenate a declining downtown.

Likewise, the *Union-Tribune* has played a significant leadership role in such quality of life issues as ensuring a water supply in an arid region, improving the world's best natural harbor, imposing strict smog controls, and building a metropolitan sewage disposal system. Among the landmark results of the Copley family's community appreciation are the downtown Copley Symphony Hall, the Copley Family YMCA, the Helen K. and James S. Copley Library in La Jolla, Copley Memorial Auditorium at the San Diego Museum of Art, and Copley Memorial Visitor Center at the Olympic Training Center.

Throughout its long history, the newspaper has helped nurture San Diego from a dusty village of 3,000 to one of the nation's largest metropolitan centers. Always true to the newspaper's founding mission, the *Union-Tribune* and the Copley family are prepared to continue a policy of aggressively reporting the issues that will affect San Diego and the nation in the coming decades.

As publisher, chairman of the board, and CEO of Copley Press, Inc., Helen K. Copley carries on her family's longtime commitment to San Diego and the Union-Tribune.

OR 122 YEARS, THE GREATER SAN DIEGO CHAMBER of Commerce has provided leadership that has improved the quality of life in San Diego. The organization has not only helped create and sustain the region's economic base, but also has assisted in shaping society, culture, the arts, and education. Since its inception, the chamber has been the community's sole ongoing leadership organization, serving as a catalyst that turns vision into reality.

"Like the seashore between the ocean and land, the chamber is always in a position to integrate two unlike entities or diverse ideas," says Lee Grissom, chamber president. "We acknowledge the inevitability of change. We resolve—and occasionally create—conflict. We experience turbulence and encourage transformation.

"We do not exist to build wealth, but without it we would have no city. From it spring civic improvements, the opera, libraries, education, the symphony, museums, zoos—all the things that make city living worthwhile."

And the chamber's record speaks for itself. In 1900, it pledged $43,000 to build the first railroad to

In December 1990, the chamber moved into the Emerald Shapery Center, the brightest jewel in the downtown San Diego skyline.

Imperial Valley. It also raised $280,000 to buy the land for what is now the Naval Training Center, led a bond drive to develop Mission Bay Park, sponsored the initial study that led to the creation of the San Diego Port District, and helped organize a bond issue that established the world-class University of California campus in San Diego.

More recently, the chamber helped bring the Super Bowl to San Diego and helped the city host the 1984 World Series, the annual Holiday Bowl and All Star Game, and two America's Cup yacht races. Heavily involved in downtown redevelopment, the chamber played a significant role in developing the city's new Convention Center and in building Horton Plaza. In 1985, the chamber acknowledged the area's significant growth northward by opening a North City branch.

BALANCING BUSINESS AND COMMUNITY INTERESTS

In all of its programs, the chamber strikes a healthy balance between business and community interests, remaining sensitive to the San Diego population as a whole. While the chamber routinely takes strong advocacy stands on business and political issues, it also takes the community's side on many controversial issues, even if they run contrary to general business interests. For instance, in 1982, the chamber prompted a criminal investigation of the county government's policy on awarding telephone contracts. It also challenged the proposed takeover of local, investor-owned San Diego Gas & Electric Co. by a Los Angeles-based, privately-owned utility, Southern California Edison—to the detriment of the chamber's own treasury.

"We believe in doing what's right for the community, taking a long-term view that will benefit everyone, including business," says Grissom.

The chamber was, however, created to be the voice of business in San Diego, serving as its advocate and ensuring that the government and other regulators consider the collective business perspective throughout San Diego County and its 18 suburban cities.

It speaks not only for the large banks, manufacturers, and industrialists, but also for medium-sized and small firms that do not have the time or funds to individually influence long-term strategic planning. The chamber's Small Business Division provides guidance, information, training, counseling, and education.

ADDRESSING A BROAD RANGE OF ISSUES

In January of 1870, a handful of merchants and bankers in the small waterfront village of San Diego organized the Chamber of Commerce in hopes of encouraging farmers to bring their crops to town for shipment abroad. To that end, the fledgling organiza-

tion worked to build a highway to Imperial Valley and improve the town's dock.

Through significant growth over the years to 3,500 member companies representing 150,000 employees, the Greater San Diego Chamber of Commerce has become one of the largest organizations of its kind in the western United States. Today, the issues before the chamber still include better transportation, improvements to the harbor, and foreign trade. But the list is now much longer: a new airport, a new sewage system, an upgraded water supply, extension of the light-rail Trolley System, county-wide metropolitan government, economic diversification, and better education.

As chamber president, Grissom is the focal point around which the organization operates, building consensus, maintaining focus, and directing its energies. Max Schetter, senior vice president and general manager of the chamber, also serves as director of the Economic Research Bureau, a unique government-funded organization that gathers business data and analyzes and interprets it for chamber members and the business community at large.

"OUR COUNTY HAS BEEN REBORN," SAYS LEE GRISSOM, CHAMBER PRESIDENT. "MANY FORCES HAVE CHANGED US PHYSICALLY, ECONOMICALLY, CULTURALLY, AND SPIRITUALLY. WE ARE CONSIDERING A NEW MOTTO: 'SAN DIEGO—WHERE THE WORLD COMES TO THINK.' "

Currently, the chamber is concerned with the leadership and public policy problems raised by estimates that the county will grow by 1.5 million people in the next 25 years. "By the year 2015, this county will likely be the home of 4 million people, the size of several states," explains Grissom. "Between now and then, the county is expected to add 750,000 new jobs and 646,000 new homes. The chamber will help to shape that future, and we want no ceiling on the potential growth. We want a sound economic floor on which such growth can be accommodated, while our leaders manage it to enhance the quality of life of everyone who lives here."

A Rebirth of San Diego

Grissom and the community leaders who serve as chamber officers point with pride to what has been called a rebirth of San Diego in recent years. The city, long viewed as only a Navy town supported by tourists, agriculture, and a military-oriented aerospace industry, has undergone significant economic change in the last decade.

The chamber called this building home from 1935 to 1967. Today, its offices are located across the street at Broadway and Columbia.

Since its founding in 1870, the chamber has remained a visible force throughout San Diego. ABOVE: The "Grand Parade" in September 1894.

"Our county has been reborn," says Grissom. "Many forces have changed us physically, economically, culturally, and spiritually. We are considering a new motto: 'San Diego—where the world comes to think.' "

Grissom cites the massive infusion of new high tech industry, universities, and researchers—both industrial and academic—that has occurred locally. The "think tanks" or "intellectual product factories" have resulted in San Diego being referred to as "the new Athens" and "Harvard's West Coast Campus."

IN ALL OF ITS PROGRAMS, THE CHAMBER STRIKES A HEALTHY BALANCE BETWEEN BUSINESS AND COMMUNITY INTERESTS, REMAINING SENSITIVE TO THE SAN DIEGO POPULATION AS A WHOLE.

"From fusion research to seismic engineering, from diagnostic medicine to freeing the world from the scourge of AIDS and cancer, from developing supercomputers to enhancing intercultural awareness and international understanding, from studying the winds and tides of El Nino to helping Astronaut Sally Ride develop a space institute on the UCSD campus—an

intellectual harvest is being gathered in this county that could shape the future," says Grissom.

One of the biggest changes in San Diego is the simultaneous growth of its sister city, Tijuana, across the Mexican border, as well as the burgeoning local population of Latinos, Asians, and African-Americans. The chamber has always maintained good relations with its business counterparts in Tijuana and for many years has had an outreach program for San Diego's minority business entrepreneurs. But demographic change in the 1980s and 1990s has mandated a new emphasis in both arenas that the chamber is prepared to meet.

"It's been said that when we look back, the things that have happened seem inevitable. When we look forward, they seem impossible. Neither, of course, is true," says Grissom. "But looking at this new intellectual community of ours, nothing seems impossible. By working together and building on the foundation of an intellectual community, San Diego has a splendid destiny."

Does the community have the leadership to take advantage of such an opportunity? Grissom believes that in two decades of change, the city has become something unique in the United States.

"We have moved away from an elitist power structure to one that is more pluralistic—a leadership structure requiring more communication, more patience, more sharing of goals, more listening, and more understanding.

"The city's leaders today are a smart, sophisticated, informed, and energetic group of men and women. I would argue that they are better informed on the options and alternatives facing our community and on world events and international business trends. They are better communicators than any group in the history of this organization."

Eight Divisions to Serve the Community

The chamber recently began operating from new downtown headquarters in the Emerald Shapery Center, one of a half dozen new high-rise structures that have dramatically lengthened and raised the city's skyline. The attractive, modern offices serve as a focal point for most chamber activities, as well as community and business groups. A full-time professional staff of 35 is divided into eight operating divisions, each of which serves a significant segment of the community.

The Military Affairs Division is the link between the region's military and defense establishment and area business and civic leaders. It serves as a lobbyist and event coordinator to help ensure that the community retains its military assets and acquires new defense contracts, while improving the quality of life for military personnel.

The Motion Picture, Television, and Arts Division assists directors and producers in filming movies on location in San Diego, thus boosting annual area income by millions of dollars, creating new jobs, and publicizing San Diego. It was one of the first such efforts in the United States.

The Small Business Development Division supports small business owners by providing seminars, training, and counseling on regulatory, government, and economic issues.

The Education Division's goal is to improve the overall quality of education in the county, with emphasis on economics and business. Its staff participates in both formulating and financing education policy.

The Government Division closely monitors local, state, national, and international affairs of government, taking strong positions on issues that affect the San Diego economy, including such recent concerns as overseas trade, downtown redevelopment, growth caps, and taxes. The chamber also acts as an advocate

on legal proposals before the City Council, County Board of Supervisors, and the State Legislature.

The Economic Research Bureau, highly regarded by the community, collects and analyzes business and economic data, and issues objective reports on local and regional trends. It is financed by the city, county, Port District, and the chamber, and its many publications help the news media, government officials, chamber members, and the general public daily.

The Communications Division provides general information to the public and the newspaper, radio, and television media on both community and business activities. It also publishes *Business Action*, the chamber's monthly member magazine and calendar of events, and annually issues hundreds of news releases and pamphlets about the community.

The Membership Division recruits and retains members by using both staff and volunteers. It also coordinates social and economic activities for its membership, providing the strength that is basic to the chamber's operations.

A Mission for the Future

The chamber's mission statement sums up its past, as well as its goals for the future: "The chamber is an action-oriented business organization dedicated to: Helping its members prosper by providing information, education, and the opportunity for networking. Promoting a positive, balanced business climate in the region by providing leadership on issues, educating members about these issues, and coalescing them and like-minded organizations into an effective force for action."

Attractive, modern offices in the Emerald Shapery Center serve as a focal point for most chamber activities.

OR WELL OVER A CENTURY — AS LONG AS ANYONE can remember—AT&T has meant telephones.

Today, it is a communications giant whose products and services constantly move an unending, worldwide river of voices, computer data, and television programs electronically—via satellites, radio, microwave, undersea cable, and fiber-optic lines.

A FULL-SERVICE INFORMATION COMPANY

American Telephone and Telegraph Co. is a full-service information company, whose firm goal is to provide the means by which any nation can access enormous data banks anywhere—backing up physicians, colleges, newspapers, scientists, industry, and business executives who need information of any type.

> AT&T CHAIRMAN ROBERT E. ALLEN SAYS THE COMPANY SOON WILL MAKE "GLOBAL COMPUTER NETWORKS AS EASY TO USE AND ACCESSIBLE AS THE TELEPHONE NETWORK IS TODAY."

Significantly, the firm has not forgotten its deep roots in phone service for the home. AT&T plans an infrastructure that will carry homework data for children, shopping information, banking transactions, and other exotic data into homes and apartments, as well as supply the home computer terminal.

AT&T's distinctive corporate headquarters is located in downtown San Diego. (Photo: Roulette Photography)

In the spring of 1991, one more piece of this global information machine fell into place. AT&T bought the giant computer manufacturer NCR Corporation for $7.4 billion, thus marrying AT&T's communications capabilities with NCR's computer design skills.

AT&T Chairman Robert E. Allen says the company soon will make "global computer networks as easy to use and accessible as the telephone network is today." AT&T will be able to tell the chief executive of a global corporation or an individual San Diego homeowner that it can provide "soup to nuts, your entire information network," including the telephone, the fax machine, a computer, and an answering machine.

INVOLVED IN SAN DIEGO SINCE 1891

AT&T's involvement in the city dates back to 1891, when a small forerunner company made it possible to call Los Angeles over newly connected local wires that had only been in place a few years. Today, its corporate headquarters are in the AT&T signature high-rise in downtown San Diego, and the telecommunications titan has operator, service, and sales facilities throughout the county.

With 2,500 local employees, including 1,400 at its NCR division, AT&T has a payroll that generates a $70 million-plus impact on the county's economy. Additionally, two sales divisions in San Diego focus on products and network services for large and small businesses. And the local International Communications Services Division, a branch of AT&T's Mexico City office, serves the communications needs of U.S. customers who have manufacturing and assembly factories in northwest Mexico.

LOCAL CULTURAL SUPPORT

A longtime supporter of the arts on a national basis, AT&T is a significant behind-the-scenes contributor to local cultural events, both experimental and traditional. In San Diego, the firm has coordinated a total of $500,000 in contributions to regional theatrical, musical, and cultural groups, including the Old Globe Theatre, San Diego Opera, La Jolla Playhouse and San Diego Repertory Theatre, and various dance companies.

Mindful that its existence depends on community satisfaction with its services, AT&T has always been a good corporate citizen, as well as a contributor to the area's economic strength.

SAN DIEGO GAS & ELECTRIC CO.

HE FIRST MAN-MADE ILLUMINATION IN SAN DIEGO was probably a Native American campfire, preceding by centuries the oil-fired lamps of exploring ship captains and the wood-burning fireplaces of the priests who founded California's first mission in 1769.

It wasn't until 1881, roughly 112 years after the San Diego de Alcalá Mission was built, that the first gas-fired street lights illuminated the dirt streets and wooden sidewalks of the San Diego village, a seaport with one rickety dock often visited by sailing ships. The town's 3,000 inhabitants saw their first electric lights in 1884, when a handful of 125-foot-tall iron towers were built to brighten entire sections of the small town.

Both sources of energy—and the wondrous marvels they wrought—were delivered by San Diego Gas & Electric, which still supplies the city with energy that lights up the night, fires the furnaces of industry, heats homes, and brings convenience into kitchens.

Today, San Diego Gas & Electric is one of the nation's largest and best managed investor-owned utilities, serving 1.1 million customers in a service territory encompassing two counties and 4,100 square miles. It has 62,000 shareholders, including a large number of San Diegans, and assets of $3.6 billion. Its annual revenues approach $2 billion.

FOUNDED BY MEN OF VISION

On June 5, 1881, *The San Diego Union* newspaper told the story of how the San Diego Gas Co. lit up the town, when the first gas-fired street lights were turned on. "Fifth Street was thronged last evening by our citizens, old and young, who had turned out to witness the novelty of the inauguration of the new gas works, and the stores and business places presented a brilliant appearance."

Two years later there were sufficient gas lines to homes for the company to advertise that gas stoves—for rent or purchase—would "save labor, expenses, worry" with "no smoke, no ashes, no dirt."

Three years after the gas plant opened, an Indiana concern started a small company to operate electric arc lights. In 1886, it was bought by two Coronado developers to supply electricity to the new Hotel del Coronado. They in turn merged with the gas company on April 15, 1887, forming the San Diego Gas, Fuel and Electric Light Co.

Founders of the gas company, who were termed "men of substance, experience, and vision" by

The South Bay Power Plant is one of two local facilities that supply SDG&E's 1.1 million electricity customers.

historians, were seven newcomers to San Diego: Dr. Robert M. Powers, Ephraim Morse, Bryant Howard, Oliver S. Witherby, George Cowles, James S. Gordon, and George W. Hazzard. These far-sighted civic leaders were also involved in founding several banks, starting a public library, creating a town park, and bringing water to the parched, semi-arid community.

MEETING COMMUNITY POWER NEEDS

SDG&E, as it is known today, is proud of a record of never failing to meet the community's power needs; its reliability is based on a diverse base of nuclear fuel, natural gas, oil, and geothermal, coal, and hydro power. It has 20 percent ownership of the nuclear plant at San Onofre.

Though it has had economic ups and downs over its 110-year history, the company is proudest of its modern-day accomplishments: continued low rates, high earnings, and customer satisfaction. For several years it has been the most cost-efficient electricity producer of all investor-owned utilities in California.

Facing change in the utility industry, including a phasing out of government regulation, SDG&E President Thomas A. Page tells his employees and the public that "the future of our company depends on building partnerships, coalitions, and allies."

"The successful new utility world will be made up of coalitions and allies working toward a common cause," he says. "We will be allies with all of the constituencies with which we do business—employees, customers, regulators, and the general public."

Built in 1911, SDG&E's Station B Power Plant continued steam and electrical service until the early 1980s.

CORONADO IS NO LONGER A SLEEPY LITTLE TOWN across the bay from San Diego.

To the surprise of longtime Southern Californians and the delight of vacationers seeking a year-round mild climate, Coronado has entered its second century as "San Diego's resort community."

A SMALL-TOWN SENSE OF COMMUNITY

Myths die hard, and residents are glad that others still perceive Coronado for what it basically is: a city of 25,000 that cherishes its small-town sense of community; its well-kept neighborhoods relatively isolated from big-city problems; its two vital Navy bases; and its abundance of single-family residences ranging in style from Victorian to post-modern.

Even though everyone calls Coronado an island, it actually is a 5.3-square-mile peninsular city, linked to San Diego by the graceful blue Coronado Bay Bridge and the Silver Strand, a narrow strip of beach that extends south to within 12 miles of Baja California, Mexico.

Until the bridge was completed in 1969, visitors used the ferry from downtown San Diego. And that suited Coronadans just fine. With its century-old main street (Orange Avenue) lined with small businesses at each end, Coronado is a lot like River City in "The Music Man." In the center of town is an old-fashioned park with a gazebo bandstand, where concerts are held every Sunday night in the summer and generations of families picnic and play.

Coronado's massive Fourth of July parade is known all along the West Coast. Every home displays a flag, the marching bands and military units stretch on for more than two hours, and spectacular military demonstrations and a fireworks display attract thousands of spectators. Christmas is another holiday

The Coronado Bay Bridge, with its graceful curve, offers sweeping views of San Diego and Coronado. (Photo: Coronado Visitor Information Bureau)

Coronadans love to share. On the first Friday of each December, five blocks of Orange Avenue are closed to traffic in the evening as merchants welcome everyone to the Christmas Open House. Residents and visitors stroll from store to store greeting old friends, sipping hot drinks, and munching on seasonal goodies.

On a single spring weekend, Coronado stages the largest indoor flower show in Southern California, the library's used book sale, and MotorCars on Main Street, an annual display of classic cars.

A FIRST-CLASS RESORT LOCATION

It was the Hotel del Coronado that put the city on the map after it opened on the beach in 1888. This grande dame of west coast resorts—with its towering red turrets and gleaming white clapboard architecture—is still thriving in its second century.

Two other full-service, international-class resorts have opened in Coronado since 1988. Le Meridien, a luxurious hotel on San Diego Bay, has quickly earned an outstanding reputation for its fine service, French cuisine, and resort amenities, which include a full-service spa, tennis facilities, and the Clarins Institut de Beaute. At the other end of town, on its own semi-private island in the bay and opposite Silver Strand State Beach, is Loews Coronado Bay Resort. Luxuriously appointed from the grand lobby to private bayside casitas, Loews has become an instant hit thanks to its attentive staff, gourmet restaurants, health club, and private boat slips.

Opened in 1888, the Hotel del Coronado is still thriving in its second century. (Photo: Hotel del Coronado)

In between are 12 other vacation properties, ranging from a bed and breakfast to a charming Mexican Colonial-style hotel housed in the former mansion of Elisha Babcock, one of the original developers of the Hotel del Coronado. Coronado also offers plenty of activities in town, as well as convenient access to San Diego attractions across the bay. The city encourages bicycling with 15 miles of paved bike paths. In addition to year-round beach access, a wealth of little-known small parks offer sensational views of the ocean and the bay. There's also free tennis at 18 city-maintained courts and golf at the beautiful and challenging municipal course. A variety of restaurants, from corner cafe to grand gourmet, complements an assortment of shops, offering everything from antiques to the ubiquitous souvenir T-shirt.

More than 100 years after its founding, Coronado is indeed the village that has it all. Its past and future are still for the taking, and its residents enthusiastically welcome everyone to their own corner in the California sun.

SAN DIEGO TRUST & SAVINGS BANK

AN DIEGO TRUST & SAVINGS BANK, THE CITY'S largest locally owned bank, operates over 50 branch banking offices and, with over 200 ATMs, one of the largest ATM networks in San Diego County. Its business strategy is based on solid banking principles established by its founding president and sustained by his successors, staff, and a large, devoted clientele. These principles represent a commitment to high productivity, continuous profitability, prudent lending, maintenance of liquidity, and cost control.

Through over 100 years of uninterrupted growth, San Diego Trust has fostered long-lasting relationships with individuals and companies, whether local, regional, or international. Refraining from acquisitions and mergers, the bank has never overextended; instead, it has always sought to develop strength from its own resources. As a result, San Diego Trust has been recognized consistently by independent financial rating organizations for its superior strength and stability among banks in the county, the state, and across the nation.

Thomas W. Sefton, grandson of the founder and former president of the bank, remarked, "Looking back, I believe it is possible to determine the intentions of our forerunners who set the course for this bank and guided it through the years...They did not enter the banking business for short-term gain. Rather, they sought a long-term commitment to San Diego based on a high quality of service."

ESTABLISHED IN 1889

Joseph W. Sefton Sr., a successful businessman from Ohio, established the bank in 1889 as San Diego Savings Bank. Confident of the city's great potential for growth, Sefton committed his wealth and talents to furthering community development. During 20 years of leadership, he developed principles of sound banking and firmly controlled the small, but growing financial institution.

A companionship developed between the two entities—community and bank—so that in 1914 San Diego Trust adopted the motto: "This City and the Bank have grown up together." Through the 1930s, San Diego Trust remained an enthusiastic supporter of community efforts to attract permanent residents and new business enterprises. Under the leadership of Joseph W. Sefton Jr., the bank's resources were marshaled to assist in the Panama-California Exposition of 1915, a milestone in San Diego's development. The bank's substantial resources also provided a solid base of support to the community during the Great Depression.

FUNDAMENTAL CHANGES IN BANKING

Over the past several decades, American banking has undergone major, fundamental changes. For example,

a tremendous increase in check transactions in the 1950s made electronic data processing (EDP) essential in the banking industry. With characteristic foresight, San Diego Trust became one of the first to adopt EDP on the West Coast.

Its use has brought countless benefits in check processing and electronic fund transfer (EFT), which includes automated teller machines (ATM) and point-of-sale (POS) computer terminals. In 1976, San Diego Trust introduced a fully operational ATM system to the community. As the first widespread application of EFT technology in the county, the ATM system further enhanced the bank's reputation for innovation.

Among the many challenges facing banks today are economic recession, soaring inflation, and regulatory action. Little regulatory activity affected the welfare of San Diego Trust during its first 20 years. But financial panics and bank failures in 1893, 1903, and 1907 forced state and federal authorities to build public confidence in banking through regulation—this at a time when San Diego Trust was known as "The Bank That Public Confidence Built."

Legislation of a different kind in 1913 enabled savings institutions to become departmental, full-service banks. In an attempt to enlarge the bank's financial activities in support of a burgeoning community, J.W. Sefton Jr. seized the opportunity to add commercial and trust departments and changed the bank's name to San Diego Trust & Savings Bank.

However, state and federal regulatory activity increased throughout the Great Depression and World War II. Not until 1978 were the first deregulatory bills finally passed, creating a dramatic increase in competition between traditional banks and non-banking entities. San Diego Trust responded by developing alternative sources of income, moving aggressively into competitive products, and providing services at prices both the bank and its clients could afford. Today, such aggressive management remains a basic element in the bank's blueprint for success.

"We plan to continue taking advantage of our superior financial strength," says Daniel D. Herde, president and CEO since 1990. "A highly trained and experienced professional staff provides us with innovative ideas and operational flexibility for a distinct competitive edge. Strength is also found in our working relationship with the community."

Founded in 1889, San Diego Trust & Savings Bank has enjoyed over a century of stability and success in San Diego. (Photo: Dale Higgins)

ONG BEFORE PAIN-PREVENTING CHLOROFORM OR disinfectants were developed for use in surgery, Mercy Hospital was caring for patients. And penicillin and other miracle drugs weren't to come along for another half century.

When the hospital was founded over 100 years ago, there were hoop skirts, horses, sailing ships, and talk of bringing a railroad to San Diego. A spectacular new structure, the gingerbread-castle Hotel Del Coronado, had just opened across the bay.

Amid all the excitement, a small notice in the weekly *San Diego Union* newspaper took note of a new infirmary on the second floor above a men's clothing store at what is now Sixth and Market streets.

"We have come to remain," Sister Mary Michael Cummings said, "and shall expect to build, in time."

RIGHT: Mother Mary Michael Cummings helped found Mercy Hospital in 1890. "We have come to remain," she said, "and shall expect to build, in time." (Photo: Mercy Hospital)

A CENTURY OF GROWTH

Sister Cummings was one of two nuns from the Ireland-based order of the Sisters of Mercy who had arrived in San Diego a few weeks before. In July 1890, with a capital investment of $50, these "advocates for the poor and those with special needs" opened a five-bed facility dedicated to the principle that everyone "has a right to quality health care."

Immediately, the Sisters began caring for patients and establishing medical precedents. From their first patient—a victim of malaria, long before there was a cure for the disease—the nuns vigorously laid the foundation for the great institution that Mercy Hospital and Medical Center has since become.

Within weeks of the hospital's opening, Dr. R.B. Hurbert performed the first recorded Caesarean section on the West Coast at the small downtown infirmary. Less than a year later, the Sisters had raised $5,000 and moved their patients to a larger facility at a site near what is now Balboa Park. The hospital moved again after a few more years to Hillcrest, located on a bluff overlooking Mission Valley, and changed its name from St. Joseph's to Mercy Hospital.

"IN SPITE OF THE DRAMATIC CHANGES AFFECTING THE HEALTH CARE INDUSTRY, WE CAN'T LOSE SIGHT OF THE FACT THAT WE'RE HERE TO CARE FOR PEOPLE," SAYS RICHARD KEYSER, PRESIDENT AND CEO. "WE ARE A COMMUNITY RESOURCE, AND PEOPLE RELY ON US FOR LIFE AND DEATH ISSUES."

A LEADING MEDICAL CENTER AND TEACHING HOSPITAL

According to banker Tom Sefton, a third generation San Diegan, "Mercy is an institution that locked hands with San Diego at the city's inception, and it has been an integral part of our town ever since, benefiting the lives of hundreds of thousands of people."

Mercy has grown into the largest private medical center in the nation's sixth largest city. In 1990, Mercy had 20,000 admissions, 285,000 outpatient visits, and 41,000 emergency room visits, and its staff made 40,000 home health care visits.

As a teaching hospital, Mercy remains committed to the continuing education and training of physicians through its highly respected Graduate Medical Education program. Since the mid-1940s, interns and residents have received post-graduate training in numerous medical specialties under the supervision of Mercy's senior medical staff. So attractive is the hospital's teaching program that it receives hundreds of applications each year from medical schools throughout the United States.

Today, the 523-bed hospital is part of a larger health care system known as Mercy Healthcare San Diego. The system includes a 194-bed skilled nursing facility, Mercy Rehabilitation and Care Center, located near the main hospital, and a network of outpatient medical facilities, Mercy Health Centers, spread throughout the county. In addition, the hospital's Foundation, its Home Care Services business, and the Mercy Magnetic Imaging Center are part of the system.

One of Mercy's most visible services to the public is the hospital's trauma center-emergency department, where specially trained medical teams meet emergency helicopters and ambulances delivering critically ill or injured patients around the clock. Of equal significance to the community are the hospital's premier medical services, which include the mercy Orthopaedic Center, Heart Institute, Neurosciences Institute, and Cancer Center.

The hospital also provides specialty care in such areas as maternal and child health, diabetes, gastroenterology, and urology. An outpatient surgical facility, area-wide preventative health services, and unique

Today, Mercy Hospital and Medical Center continues to build on its founding commitment to serving the San Diego community. (Photo: Mercy Hospital)

membership programs for seniors, Hispanics, and women round out Mercy's slate of offerings. And at Mercy Clinic, physicians treat more than 30,000 low income patients every year—a visible example of the hospital's commitment to its founding mission.

Nearing the 100th anniversary of the hospital, the *San Diego Union* editorialized that the facility has been "the portal for many San Diegans entering the world and has kept others in good health, solid proof that this *grande dame* of health care has played a significant role in the city's history."

"No other private hospital in San Diego attempts to provide the special clinical services for the poor...as well as the doctor training and other obligations that

Mercy believes are central to the healing mission of the Sisters of Mercy," added the *Los Angeles Times*.

TACKLING THE HIGH COST OF QUALITY HEALTH CARE

For years, hospital administrators have faced the challenge of balancing funds to care for the needy. The problem has intensified over the last decade, as the nation's health care system has undergone change brought about by public cries for lower medical costs and legislative action.

"We are in the forefront of technological change," says Richard Keyser, Mercy president and chief executive officer. "Increasingly sophisticated technology has brought about advances in lifesaving and life-prolonging devices and medications.

"At the same time, with each medical breakthrough, we find the accompanying problem of how to cover the costs of these advances. For example, new trauma centers have lowered the number of preventable deaths from 33 to 1 percent in San Diego, but maintaining helicopters and staffing teams of highly skilled doctors and nurses are very expensive."

Regarding Mercy's commitment to offering quality care and balancing costs, Keyser cites the creed of the hospital's founders: "What we have, we hold in trust for others. As Sisters of Mercy, our hope is that we can challenge ourselves and all who collaborate with us to be truly 'of mercy.'"

"It is this value system that has carried us through over a century of service," explains Keyser. "In spite of the dramatic changes affecting the health care industry, we can't lose sight of the fact that we're here to care for people. We are a community resource, and people rely on us for life and death issues."

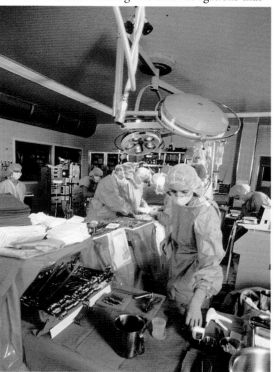

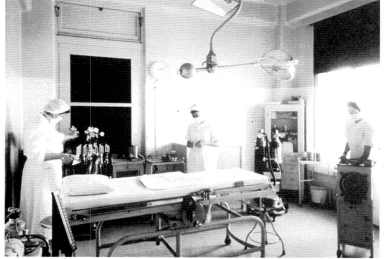

Surgical facilities at Mercy have undergone dramatic change from the early days (below) to today's state-of-the-art operating suites (below left). (Photos: Mercy Hospital)

CITY OF CHULA VISTA

LESSED WITH A MAGNIFICENT HARBOR, ROLLING foothills, and pristine lakes, Chula Vista offers the diversity and charm that is Southern California. The city features a harbor with new marinas, bayside parks, and restaurants; a world-class U.S. Olympic Training Center under construction; a colorful and quaint village-style downtown; and exciting new master-planned communities with housing ranging from condominiums and townhouses to spacious lakeside and fairway homes.

Chula Vista enjoys a unique international setting, serving as the gateway to the Pacific Rim and Mexico. In fact, it is only seven miles via Interstates 5 and 805 from the U.S./Mexican border—the busiest border in the world. And San Diego International Airport is just 10 miles to the north.

> CHULA VISTA HAS CAUGHT THE OLYMPIC SPIRIT! THE NATION'S THIRD OFFICIAL OLYMPIC TRAINING CENTER WILL OPEN ON THE SHORE OF OTAY LAKES IN 1993.

More than 130 bird species can be viewed from the Chula Vista Nature Interpretive Center in the bayfront's Sweetwater Marsh National Wildlife Refuge.

With a population of more than 140,000, Chula Vista is San Diego County's second largest city. Reflecting the diversity of a 21st century city, the community is home to 44 percent of all business in San Diego County's South Bay region, including Rohr, Inc., a Fortune 500 company, and Nellcor, a high tech manufacturer.

Chula Vista welcomes business. *City and State* magazine's "Annual Financial Report of the 50 Up and Coming Cities" calls Chula Vista one of "the centers to watch in the 1990s" based upon the city's exceptional fiscal and economic vigor. An active economic development program and Redevelopment Agency assist business and facilitate desirable economic growth. Successful redevelopment projects have ranged from downtown decorative streetscaping to expansion and upgrading of Chula Vista Center

regional mall to the addition of the new Superior Courts.

A CASUAL, OUTDOORS LIFESTYLE

Chula Vista's near-perfect Mediterranean climate lends itself to a casual, outdoors lifestyle. Throughout the year, residents enjoy such pastimes as sailing and windsurfing on the bay, hiking in nearby deserts and mountains, and fishing in freshwater lakes and the Pacific Ocean.

Chula Vista Harbor is the southern home port for the state's official tall ship, the *Californian*, and is headquarters for the Chula Vista Yacht Club, challenger for the Little America's Cup in 1991. The Chula Vista Nature Interpretive Center spotlights one of the few remaining natural saltwater marshes on the entire California coast, offering rare looks at more than 130 species of birds and wetlands ecology.

In 1993, a new Olympic Training Center will open in Chula Vista on the western shore of Otay Lakes. Visitors will be able to watch future U.S. Olympians train in archery, canoeing, diving, soccer, track and field, field hockey, rowing, tennis, and other warm-weather sports.

COMMITTED TO QUALITY GROWTH

To maintain a desirable quality of life for its residents, Chula Vista has become one of the most progressive cities in Southern California and a leader in growth management. A model Growth Management Plan ensures that residential development is accompanied by needed capital facilities and services. "Threshold" standards for community needs such as parks, schools, water, and streets are monitored yearly to guarantee that the city's standards of excellence are maintained.

Adding to this quality of life are such facilities as Southwestern Community College, three major hospitals with an additional 400-bed facility being planned, three golf courses, bike paths and equestrian trails, a planned golf resort hotel, and a proposed lagoon-oriented $500 million mixed-use resort complex with a cultural arts center crowning the bay.

Chula Vista is right on track with well-laid plans to ensure that the city continues as a terrific place to live and work—now and into the next century.

Master-planned neighborhoods in Chula Vista feature a variety of contemporary housing and amenities.

1900-1929

1919

SAN DIEGO CONVENTION AND VISITORS BUREAU

1921

PARDEE CONSTRUCTION COMPANY

1924

SCRIPPS INSTITUTIONS OF MEDICINE AND SCIENCE

1927

GRAY, CARY, AMES & FRYE

1927

SHEPPARD, MULLIN, RICHTER & HAMPTON

1927

SOLAR TURBINES INCORPORATED

1929

KELCO DIVISION OF MERCK & CO., INC.

PARDEE CONSTRUCTION COMPANY

FOUNDED IN 1921 BY GEORGE M. PARDEE SR. AS A custom home-building company, Pardee Construction Company is today one of the nation's leading developers of master-planned communities.

A Weyerhauser company since 1969, Pardee has made home ownership a reality for more than 32,000 families in Southern California and Nevada. Headquartered in Los Angeles with offices in San Diego, Riverside, and Las Vegas, Pardee employs approximately 375 people.

MASTER-PLANNED COMMUNITIES A HALLMARK

President and Chief Executive Officer David E. Landon and Executive Vice President and Chief Operating Officer Vance T. Meyer have made master-planned communities the hallmark of Pardee's success throughout Southern California. During the past decade, the concept of master-planned communities has taken the company to new heights of planning and building achievement in San Diego.

Sabre Springs, a 1,500-acre master-planned community tucked in the hills west of Poway, received an "Orchid Award" for its sensitive integration into the environment. The community's scenic setting, combined with its convenient location along Interstate 15 and Poway Road, has made Pardee's 50-acre Sabre Springs Business Park one of San Diego's most sought after corporate locations. In fact, such nationally known companies as Scientific Atlanta and Herco Technology have relocated large operations to the park. The natural beauty of the area, a top-rated school district, convenient shopping, and excellent location attract families and businesses alike to Sabre Springs.

Ranked as one of San Diego's best business locations, Pardee's 102-acre San Diego Corporate Center is situated along Interstate 5 just east of Del Mar. Home to such firms as Fujitsu Systems of

> **SABRE SPRINGS, A 1,500-ACRE COMMUNITY TUCKED IN THE HILLS WEST OF POWAY, WON AN "ORCHID AWARD" FOR PLANNING EXCELLENCE.**

America, Management Analysis Corporation, Scripps Memorial Hospital Medical Offices, and Laser Power Optics, the center serves as a gateway to Pardee's 1,400-acre Del Mar Highlands community on Del Mar Heights Road. Residents enjoy a quality working and living environment, which includes parks, schools, shopping centers, many public facilities, and recreational areas.

DECADES OF MASTER-PLANNING SUCCESS

In 1969, Pardee began its first master-planned community in San Diego with Mira Mesa. Today, families continue to be attracted to Mira Mesa because of its range of housing options, from homes priced for the first-time buyer to upscale homes for the move-up buyer.

More recently, the emergence of bi-national commerce with Mexico has focused Pardee's attention on Otay Mesa. Located near the U.S.-Mexico border along Interstate 905, an 800-acre community of homes, commercial facilities, and an office park is planned.

With the success of its communities in San Diego County firmly established, Pardee is beginning a new era of master-planning with Cottonwood Hills, a 1,969-acre community near Lake Elsinore. Located amid the hillsides and valleys of southwest Riverside County, this newest development will provide housing for approximately 11,415 residents.

As it looks to the 21st century, Pardee remains committed to the master-planning concept. Its ability to offer Southern Californians quality-built homes and carefully conceived, environmentally sensitive communities is likely to ensure the firm's continued success and its solid reputation.

Sabre Springs' natural beauty and a top-rated school district continue to draw families to the community, where residents enjoy scenic walks along Chicarita Creek.

Pardee Center, an office complex of five elegant buildings, sits at the threshold of San Diego Corporate Center in Del Mar Highlands.

For many Californians, kelp forms the lush green forests which provide deep sea divers a canopy under which to explore. For beach goers, kelp is the pile of brown weeds that washes up after a coastal storm. But to Kelco, giant kelp *(Macrocystis Pyrefira)* is a precious natural resource which the company manufactures into alginates for food and industrial uses.

The use of kelp as a source of algin to manufacture drugs was discovered in 1883 by a British pharmacist. The technology was eventually applied to California's enormous kelp beds in 1927 by Fred C. Thornley, whose Kelp Products Company extracted the algin for use in a can-sealing compound. In 1929, Arnold Fitger and a group of Los Angeles-based investors purchased the company and renamed it Kelco.

As a renewable resource, kelp is harvested much as a lawn is mowed. Specially designed ships move slowly along the California coast, trimming the top three feet off strands of buoyant kelp. Owned by the state, the beds are harvested under the supervision of the California Department of Fish and Game. Almost daily, the wet kelp is collected and delivered to a 26-acre waterfront manufacturing plant near the Coronado Bridge. There, the kelp is chopped, washed, cooked, and clarified to remove impurities. The algin is then recovered, dried, milled, and packaged for shipment.

Giant kelp is a precious natural resource which Kelco manufactures into alginates for food and industrial uses and pharmaceutical and cosmetic applications.

Today, these naturally occurring alginates are used to stabilize ice cream during temperature variations (from the grocery store to a home freezer) and as gelling agents in bakery fillings, puddings, and sauces. Alginates have pharmaceutical and cosmetic applications as well, including use in tablet disintegrants, dental impression compounds, and antacid formulations.

The stabilizing characteristics of the alginates are also desirable in paper coating and sizing. Used in textile printing and dyeing, alginates help control the ink consistency on intricately patterned fabrics and carpets, in everyday clothing, and in commercial floor coverings.

COMMITTED TO DISCOVERING NEW PRODUCTS

In the mid-1950s, Kelco broadened its scope by entering a related field—culturing bacteria to make a variety of new products called biogums. The most important of these is xanthan gum, a substance which touches people's lives every day.

Like alginates, the gum is naturally occurring and water soluble, but has more diverse uses in foods. Kelco has pioneered its use in that area, from dressings and chocolate syrup to shampoo and toothpaste. Kelco has also discovered that xanthan gum is an ideal thickener and suspending agent in industrial and oil field drilling fluids. As a result, the company is the world's leading producer of xanthan gum.

Since 1980, Kelco has cultured natural organisms in search of other useful gums. The company's microbiologists recently introduced gellan gum to the food market. This revolutionary substance enhances texture and acts as a gelling agent in foods exposed to extreme changes in temperature. Rhamsan gum was introduced for industrial uses in cleaners and paints, and welan gum was made available for oil field drilling fluids and as an anti-washout additive for such underwater concrete structures as pier pilings.

AN INTERNATIONAL COMPANY WITH LOCAL IMPACT

In 1972, Kelco became a division of Merck & Co., Inc., a major international pharmaceutical organization with 37,000 employees and research and manufacturing facilities in 18 countries.

Today, Kelco operates 19 facilities worldwide from its San Diego headquarters. With sales offices in most major cities across the globe, the company maintains five manufacturing plants—San Diego; Okmulgee, Oklahoma; Knowsley, England; and Barcaldine and Girvan, Scotland.

In addition to its global reach, Kelco has a significant impact on the local economy. Of its 1,400 employees, 625 are based in San Diego and generate a $24 million annual payroll. Likewise, Kelco's purchase of local goods and services totals over $32 million annually.

It is doubtful that the scientists who founded the company in 1929 could have envisioned the scientific and commercial contributions that today's Kelco makes to society; but the basic research goals those pioneers set in the laboratory are still the guiding principles of the company. Their commitment to applied research on behalf of customer problem-solving is the backbone of Kelco's history of success.

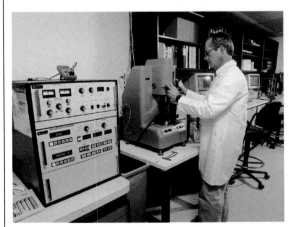

Applied research on behalf of customer problem-solving is the backbone of Kelco's history of success. LEFT: Scientists conduct rheology testing in one of Kelco's laboratories. (Photo: Ferrari Productions)

SCRIPPS INSTITUTIONS OF MEDICINE AND SCIENCE

HE MOST IMPORTANT AND BEAUTIFUL GIFT ONE human being can give to another is, in some way, to make life a little better to live."

With those words, two-thirds of a century ago, philanthropist Ellen Browning Scripps founded a small hospital and clinic in San Diego's sea coast village of La Jolla. Today, the name Scripps is instantly recognized in medical circles around the world as a synonym for quality medicine, scientific discovery, disease prevention, and professional and community education.

Scripps Institutions of Medicine and Science, founded on the simple premise of improving life, today is a diverse health organization. Integrating hospital-based, private, and group practice physicians with world-class researchers, Scripps provides comprehensive medical care and a broad range of community services.

Scripps is the largest health care institution in San Diego County. Its four hospitals, network of regional clinics, and research institute make it the county's second largest non-government employer. Services at its nonprofit facilities range from technologically advanced trauma care and organ transplantation to sophisticated cancer treatment and cutting-edge biomedical research.

As a tertiary care facility, Scripps physicians treat everything from a mundane head cold to the most critical, life-threatening disease. With an annual budget of approximately $750 million, Scripps employs 7,200 people and has 1,800 affiliated physicians.

> "WE HAVE A SYSTEM THAT IS DELIVERING THE MOST ADVANCED TECHNOLOGIES AND THE HIGHEST MEDICAL EXPERTISE," SAYS PRESIDENT AND CHIEF EXECUTIVE OFFICER CHARLES C. EDWARDS, M.D. "IT'S A POOLING OF RESOURCES AND KNOWLEDGE, TRANSLATING RESEARCH INTO CLINICAL PRACTICE."

Scripps' blending of researchers with hands-on physician specialists in a not-for-profit grouping of hospitals and clinics has created what many medical professionals believe is one of the premier medical specialty institutions on the West Coast. "We have a system that is delivering the most advanced technologies and the highest medical expertise," says President and Chief Executive Officer Charles C. Edwards, M.D. "It's a pooling of resources and knowledge, translating research into clinical practice."

"A PERSON OF GREAT VISION"

Ellen Browning Scripps was 87 years old, recuperating from a broken hip, when the idea for a hospital came to her in 1924. The sister and business partner of Edward W. Scripps (of newspaper chain fame), she donated both land and money to the venture. That year, the 44-bed Scripps Memorial Hospital opened. Her vision for a nearby clinic, also founded in 1924, was that the public would benefit from an institution specifically based on clinical medicine, research, and education.

"She was a person of great vision, a risk-taker who was not afraid to create medical facilities in the farthest corner of the U.S. at a time when it was one of the most remote," says Executive Vice President and Chief Operating Officer Ames Early. "She would be pleased with the accomplishments we've made in 68 years, very pleased indeed."

Scripps Institutions of Medicine and Science today consists of three separate operating entities: Scripps Memorial Hospitals, Scripps Clinic and Research Foundation, and The Scripps Research Institute.

SCRIPPS MEMORIAL HOSPITALS

Scripps Memorial Hospitals consists of four acute care hospitals, surrounded by specialty medical centers that not only diagnose and treat patients, but also conduct basic medical research, operate disease prevention programs, and hold a variety of medical symposiums—all unusual activities for not-for-profit community hospitals. Scripps Memorial is involved in a broad spectrum of medicine through major facilities with such specialties as cancer and arrhythmia treatment, open heart and laser surgery, high technology eye care, and chemical dependency.

Scripps boasts a Nobel Laureate researching diabetes and specialty trauma teams that hourly meet

This multifaceted, 476-bed facility in La Jolla's Golden Triangle is the Scripps Memorial centerpiece, where a medical staff of more than 1,200 offers diagnosis and treatment in more than 50 fields of medicine and surgery.

helicopters bringing in emergency accident victims. There are also two convalescent hospitals, several medical office buildings, and three highly popular health information and education centers operated by The WELL BEING program.

Growth in La Jolla eventually forced the original hospital to move to its present site, a 43-acre campus-like setting on Genesee Avenue in the Golden Triangle. This multifaceted, 476-bed institution is the Scripps Memorial centerpiece, which includes the freestanding 88-bed McDonald Center for Alcoholism and Drug Addiction Treatment, the 44,000-square-foot Whittier Institute, and the new Schaetzel Center for Health Education. A medical staff of more than 1,200 offers diagnosis and treatment in more than 50 fields of medicine and surgery.

The 150-bed Scripps Memorial Hospital in Encinitas is meeting the needs of San Diego's North County area, one of the fastest-growing areas in the United States.

Up the coast about 12 miles is the Scripps Memorial Hospital in Encinitas. The rapidly expanding 150-bed facility houses the 33-bed Rehabilitation Center, which serves patients with severe catastrophic disabilities. The hospital, acquired in 1978, is meeting the needs of San Diego's North County area, one of the fastest-growing areas in the United States. Other special services include an outpatient Surgery Center, a 24-hour Emergency Center, and the Cancer Center.

Scripps Memorial Hospital in Chula Vista, about 15 miles south of San Diego, is a 159-bed facility that was acquired in 1986. It has a surgicenter, a 20-bed obstetrical unit, a 10-bed neonatal intensive care nursery, and a full emergency services department. An expansion onto 8.9 acres of land adds a new advanced medical facility to the west of the existing hospital tower, a new medical office building, and a more efficient traffic and parking system.

Scripps Memorial Hospitals also operates Green Hospital of Scripps Clinic. Complementing the acute care facilities are the 161-bed Torrey Pines Convalescent Hospital in La Jolla and the 99-bed Ocean View Convalescent Hospital in Encinitas. Scripps also operates The Whittier Institute for Diabetes and Endocrinology, located on the La Jolla campus, which was established in 1980 for research, education, and treatment. Among its distinguished staff is Roger Guillemin, M.D., a Nobel Laureate, who supervises a staff of 35 scientists.

Major specialty centers within Scripps include the Stevens Cancer Center, Cardiovascular Institute, Mericos Eye Institute, Behavioral Medicine Department (comprised of the Pain Center, the Mental Health Center, and The McDonald Center), Cardiac

Treatment Center, Neurodiagnostic and Hearing Center, Regional Cardiac Arrhythmia Center, and the Rehabilitation Center. The hospital's affiliated health programs are Home Health Care Services and Home Medical Equipment, Center for Weight Management, and The Center for Executive Health. Scripps is also a provider of innovative community service programs, including HealthCareFinder, a physician and health service referral program; Health-Plus55, which coordinates health care and provides general assistance and screenings for people over 55; and Women's Health Source, which aims at easing access to health services for women.

The WELL BEING health program, created in 1981, operates education and information resource centers at three major shopping centers in La Jolla, Encinitas, and Chula Vista. Health seminars, classes, and screenings for the general public are held, with about 550 different courses available each year. The program also answers tens of thousands of general health questions and distributes a similar number of pamphlets.

SCRIPPS CLINIC AND RESEARCH FOUNDATION
In medical circles throughout the world, the term "Scripps Clinic in La Jolla" evokes respect, reverence, and honor. As one of the oldest nonprofit private medical centers in the United States, Scripps Clinic and Research Foundation provides comprehensive medical care for the family, distinguished physician education, and sophisticated biomedical research.

Founded in 1924, Scripps Clinic has maintained a time-honored commitment to advancing the art of medicine and preserving health, while simultaneously treating illness. The institution has treated artists, scientists, and some of the world's political, government, and religious leaders. But its strong regional base of patients also receives expert, compassionate care.

Green Hospital of Scripps Clinic is a 173-bed acute care facility located on the 46-acre Torrey Pines main campus.

The 300 physician members of the Scripps Clinic Medical Group offer diagnosis and treatment in 50 fields of medicine and surgery. In 1991 alone, physicians logged almost 600,000 patient visits. They provide comprehensive medical services by treating common illnesses, as well as complex and life-threatening diseases.

On its 46-acre Torrey Pines main campus overlooking the Pacific Ocean is the 173-bed Green Hospital of Scripps Clinic, an acute care facility and one of the Scripps Memorial Hospitals, and the Anderson Outpatient Pavilion, which provides primary and specialty care for ambulatory patients. Scripps Clinic also operates a network of regional medical facilities throughout San Diego County.

Specialty units at Scripps Clinic include the Weingart Center for Bone Marrow Transplantation; San Diego County's only Liver Transplantation Program; the Green Cancer Center; the Stone Treatment Center, which utilizes a non-surgical lithotripter for kidney stones; the Musculoskeletal Center; the Heart, Lung and Vascular Center; the Sleep Disorders Center; the Diabetes Center; the Fertility Center; the Neurosciences Center; the Pain Treatment Center; the W.M. Keck Foundation Autoimmune Disease Center; the Sports Medicine

"OUR VISION IS FOR AN EFFICIENT, COST-EFFECTIVE OPERATION, ONE THAT REFLECTS THE EVOLVING MEDICAL CLIMATE, BUT ONE THAT RESPONDS TO THE MEDICAL COMMUNITY AND PATIENT NEEDS AS WELL," SAYS EXECUTIVE VICE PRESIDENT AND CHIEF OPERATING OFFICER AMES EARLY. "IT MUST BE A COHERENT WHOLE, A CONTINUUM OF CARE, FROM BASIC RESEARCH TO CARE AND PREVENTION. NOT MANY SYSTEMS HAVE SUCCESSFULLY ACHIEVED THIS RANGE OF SERVICE."

Center; the Shiley Sports and Health Center; a facility for comprehensive radiologic and imaging diagnoses; and one of the nation's top vascular laboratories. Two of Scripps Clinic's specialty units—the Asthma and Allergic Diseases Center and the General Clinical Research Center—have been designated by the U.S. government's National Institutes of Health as facilities where experimental therapies are given clinical trials.

Another integral and vital component of Scripps Clinic is its educational programs for physicians and surgeons. Through the Department of Academic Affairs, Scripps Clinic is a nationally accredited sponsor of continuing medical education and holds more than 40 medical education conferences each year. Academic Affairs also administers clinical residency and fellowship programs for physicians. The wide range of programs sponsored by the department ensures that members of the clinical and research staffs, as well as health care professionals outside of Scripps Clinic, remain current on advances in medicine and biomedical research.

As part of its commitment to education, Scripps Clinic also sponsors numerous seminars, workshops, and classes for the public on a variety of health topics. Through the Health Resource Center at the Shiley Sports and Health Center, programs are offered in weight management, nutrition, smoking cessation, stress management, breast health, breastfeeding, parenting, injury prevention, and exercise. In addition, a series of free lectures is presented to the community each fall and spring by leading physicians at Scripps Clinic.

THE SCRIPPS RESEARCH INSTITUTE

On the same Torrey Pines campus is The Scripps Research Institute, the world's largest nonprofit biomedical research facility not affiliated with a university. Headed by Richard A. Lerner, M.D., president of The Scripps Research Institute and one of the Institute's five members of the National Academy of Sciences, the staff includes 1,200 principal investigators, postdoctoral fellows, technicians, and support staff. The Institute's annual budget of more than $80 million is derived primarily from the National

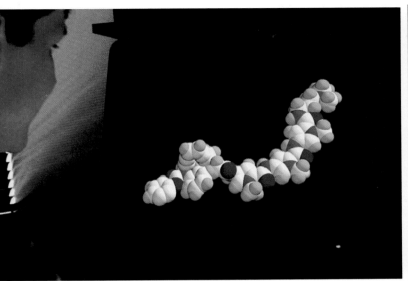

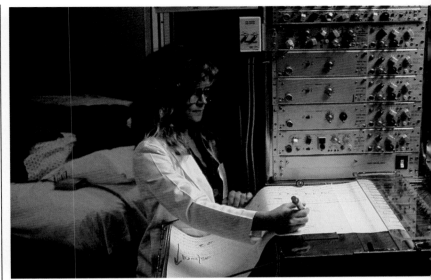

Institutes of Health and other federal agencies. The Scripps Research Institute is divided into six departments: Cell Biology, Chemistry, Immunology, Molecular Biology, Molecular and Experimental Medicine, and Neuropharmacology. A Department of Neurobiology will be added in 1992, to be headed by Nobel Laureate Gerald M. Edelman, M.D., Ph.D.

Research is conducted in several modern laboratory buildings, including the Stein Clinical Research Center, the Immunology Building, and the Molecular Biology Building. In addition, a Chemistry Center is being planned for the Lita Annenberg Hazen Science Center on the new Lusk Research Campus.

Clinical researchers and scientists work together to understand, control, treat, and ultimately prevent heart problems, strokes, cancer, arthritis, and other autoimmune diseases, as well as viral disorders, kidney dysfunction, alcoholism, chemical abuse, and multiple sclerosis.

One of the more significant successes in recent years was the development and testing of a potent anti-leukemia drug, known as 2-CdA (2-Chloro-deoxyadenosine). Thanks to the efforts of scientists and clinicians, the drug is currently keeping hundreds of hairy-cell leukemia patients alive. This achievement has often been cited as an example of the close ties between researchers and physicians.

Other accomplishments in the last decade include the following: the synthesis of a complete form of surfactant, an essential lung material that keeps air sacs open and prevents respiratory distress syndrome, a major killer of adults and premature babies; development of a new method to make disease-fighting proteins called monoclonal antibodies; the first clinical tests using a monoclonal antibody/drug conjugate to treat lung cancer; a determination by X-ray crystallography of a complete three-dimensional molecular structure of the polio virus; and the cloning

of the gene for the enzyme that is deficient in Gaucher's disease, followed by the development of a method to predict the severity of the disease.

MEETING FUTURE CHALLENGES IN MEDICINE AND HEALTH CARE

As the Scripps Institutions look to the future, they face a volatile era in which basic medical economics are changing—in which the nation's delivery of medical care is being questioned. Scripps executives believe their plans and decisions are breaking new ground toward meeting those challenges.

"As the new century approaches, our current response to change in the health care industry may well be viewed not only as a turning point in the history of the Scripps organizations, but as a model by which other organizations may measure their effectiveness and adaptability in the years ahead," says Edwards.

"Our vision is for an efficient, cost-effective operation, one that reflects the evolving medical climate, but one that responds to the medical community and patient needs as well," states Early. "It must be a coherent whole, a continuum of care from basic research to treatment and prevention. Not many systems have successfully achieved this range of service."

"With a very committed group of physicians, scientists, donors, and volunteers, we are confident in our ability to move this institution into the next century to fulfill our mission of treating illness and ultimately curing disease," says Edwards. "We fully expect extraordinary accomplishment and achievement in improving the human condition."

OLAR TURBINES INCORPORATED, HEADQUARTERED on the city's downtown waterfront, is a major element of San Diego's economic backbone. It is the city's largest exporter of manufactured goods and one of its largest employers. Solar employees, numbering 3,000 locally in two manufacturing plants and another 1,200 in 30 offices and plants worldwide, are continuing a heritage of sophisticated production that began in 1927.

The company builds a family of powerful gas turbine engines, natural gas compressors, and electricity-producing generator sets that primarily serve industrial needs. In fact, Solar is the world's leading manufacturer of industrial gas turbines ranging up to 25,000 horsepower, with more than 8,500 currently in service in 70 nations. Year in and year out, Solar exports over 70 percent of its products.

"Historically, the company has been a major factor in San Diego's economy," says Max Schetter, San Diego Chamber of Commerce vice president for economic research. "In addition to its huge payroll, Solar has an emotional, cultural, and civic bond to the community that goes back almost two-thirds of a century."

"Solar also does a lot for the community's economy indirectly," says Dan Pegg, president of the San Diego Economic Development Corporation. "Solar employs mostly highly skilled technicians and engineers, but Solar also provides entry-level opportunities that can be upgraded by in-house and external training, contributing to San Diego's skilled labor pool."

Over the past five years, Solar and its employees, combined with the Caterpillar Foundation, have contributed nearly $3 million to support more than 150 San Diego community service organizations. In addition to financial contributions, Solar employees volunteer about 16,500 hours per year on community service projects ranging from literacy programs to helping the homeless through the Solar Turbines Employees' Volunteer Club.

In terms of taxes, payroll, and local purchase of goods and services, Solar employees have an impact on the community of roughly $500 million a year—a long way from the handful of engineers and mechanics who, in 1927, had the courage, imagination, and skills to build one of the world's first metal airplanes.

OWNED BY CATERPILLAR INC.
Solar is today owned by Caterpillar Inc. of Peoria, Illinois. The world's largest manufacturer of earthmoving, construction, mining, and materials handling equipment and a major manufacturer of diesel and natural gas engines, Caterpillar has 60,000 employees worldwide.

In recent years, Caterpillar has invested $187 million in capital improvements at Solar's San Diego operations and plans to spend another $100 million to further upgrade the waterfront facility before 1998. This degree of commitment strengthens Solar's impact upon the San Diego economy, while creating the foundation for increased business.

Caterpillar has also made a substantial investment in Solar's manufacturing process. For example, the company's computer-controlled machinery produces precision, quality metal components. Solar's computer-aided design equipment has helped boost the company's position as an innovator in minimizing exhaust emissions from its engines and in designing advanced heat-exchangers to conserve energy.

A VARIETY OF INNOVATIVE PRODUCTS
Solar's key products are industrial gas turbine engines from 1,340 to 14,100 horsepower; natural gas compressors; gas turbine-driven compressor sets and mechanical drive packages; and generator sets with electrical outputs ranging from one to 10 megawatts. The company also makes a variety of advanced steam generators (boilers) and some specialized products for the U.S. military.

Solar pioneered the concept of factory-packaged small industrial gas turbines in 1960, when it introduced the 1,000-horsepower Saturn engine in generator sets and gas compressor sets. By 1990, the company had manufactured more than 8,500 industrial turbomachinery packages, which is nearly double the total from any other manufacturer. The units have logged 350 million operating hours—a level of experience equivalent to almost 40,000 years.

Solar builds several models in three basic gas turbine families, (front to rear) Saturn®, Centaur®, and Mars®.

Skilled, dedicated employees at Solar are a key factor contributing to the company's leadership and success.

Most of Solar's products are used in the oil and gas industry for production, processing, and pipeline transmission of natural gas and crude oil. A growing number of customers, however, are using Solar equipment to produce energy for their own plants and processes—simultaneously generating electricity, while using the turbine's exhaust heat for processing applications in the production of pharmaceuticals, chemicals, and food products. Another major portion of its client base utilizes Solar generator sets that supply fixed-base electrical power or emergency backup power for vital telecommunications complexes and computer centers.

Solar's research and development takes place in-house. With an international sales organization, local manufacturing and shipping, worldwide on-site installation, follow-up customer service operations, and a global parts distribution network, Solar is a fully integrated operation.

Solar's San Diego facilities consist of:
♦ The 700,000-square-foot world headquarters facility sitting alongside San Diego Harbor and adjacent to Lindbergh Field. Bounded by Harbor Drive, Pacific Highway, and Laurel and Grape streets, Solar's waterfront buildings house research, engineering, development testing, component manufacturing, and executive and administrative functions.
♦ The 300,000-square-foot Kearny Mesa plant, which houses the gas compressor manufacturing unit, gas turbine assembly, assembly of complete gas compressor sets, generator sets and mechanical-drive packages, and final product testing and shipping.
♦ The 50,000-square-foot Sky Park Court facility, housing application engineering, package engineering, project engineering, and construction services offices.

Other major operations include a division producing modules for the oil and gas industry in Texas, several large overhaul centers in Texas, Canada, Belgium, Indonesia, Malaysia, Australia, and Mexico, and a component re-manufacturing plant in Mexico. Sales and service offices are located throughout the world.

ORIGINS IN AIRCRAFT MANUFACTURING

Solar began as an aircraft manufacturing company inspired by the excitement in the aviation and metal industries after Charles Lindbergh's successful transatlantic flight in May 1927. In fact, Lindbergh's plane was built in what is today part of Solar's waterfront plant.

Though Solar built only three airplanes, the new technology and skills that evolved put the company at the forefront of a new industry, making specialty metal products for the fledgling aviation industry. After many variations and numerous market and economic changes, Solar's expertise led the company toward its current speciality—making sophisticated metal turbines to supply the world with energy.

The aircraft company was housed in a 10,000-square-foot shop in a vacant fish cannery where Juniper Street abruptly ends at the harbor. Next door was the aircraft company that built Lindbergh's *Spirit of St. Louis*.

Over the years, components produced for the U.S. military in the ever-expanding plant helped America in many wars—cold and hot. There were stainless steel exhaust manifolds and other parts for fighter planes and bombers, water desalting equipment for

Solar gas turbines are built and tested at the Kearny Mesa plant. Complete gas turbine packages are also assembled here.

ships, and portable electrical generator sets to operate military radar equipment and missile controls.

Solar's trouble-shooting research also helped avoid problems commonly developed during battle. For example, Solar engineers—working without fee—solved high altitude metal fatigue problems on engine parts of the World War II P-38 fighter. They later did similar research for the U.S. War Department on other aircraft. The engineering know-how and design techniques developed by Solar research laboratories contributed to the company's leadership role in manufacturing durable, specialty high temperature metal structures. Solar's expertise also prepared the company for its prosperous future in turbines.

STABILITY THROUGH DIVERSITY AND EMPLOYEE COMMITMENT

Over the years, through economic downturns, the Great Depression, and occasional recessions, the firm turned out such items as metal frying pans, book ends, popsicle trays, kitchen sinks, midget race car bodies, coffee brewers, stainless steel caskets, and—for a short time—redwood lawn chairs. Because of this versatility, Solar was able to make a postwar transition from military to industrial product lines.

Edmund T. Price, Solar's president from shortly after the company's inception until his 1956 retirement, once told a newspaper reporter a Depression-era story that continues to epitomize the spirit of the company's employees. In 1932, during the darkest days of the Depression, "we had no money to meet the payroll. We owed money to the banks. I walked

out into the shop and told the men I was sorry, but it was the end of the line. We were closing up.

"Ironically, that morning we had received an order for 126 exhaust manifolds for the Boeing 247 transport. It was a $26,000 order, but we had no money to meet the payroll so we had to close.

"The men listened with serious faces. There was silence for a minute after I had finished speaking. Then Bill James spoke up. 'What the hell are we waiting for,' he said. He took off his coat and walked over to his bench. The other men followed. We were still in business."

For several weeks, every man worked without pay to preserve the company. Those workers are still remembered today. Solar's employee-built all faith chapel on the grounds of the Harbor Drive plant is open at all times. Someone is often inside, reading a bible, saying a prayer, or just sitting in contemplation. There are weekly, non-denominational services during lunch or work breaks.

Outside, there's an open air dining and recreation area where a bronze plaque commemorates Bill James, who led his fellow employees back to work: "In memory of W.A. James, drop hammer operator in 1932, who had faith in his team."

Solar attributes its success over the years to the dedication of its employees. The company is committed to providing a work place that is safe and pleasant, one that promotes growth, opportunity, teamwork, and reward.

Today, self-directed work teams are currently striving to solve problems and bring new ideas to the

A 14,100-horsepower Mars mechanical drive unit powers a centrifugal gas compressor on this Solar-engineered package at a gas processing plant.

Thousands of employees at Solar contribute unique, individual skills that enable the company to produce and support products that customers can rely upon to meet their energy needs.

forefront at Solar. These teams are encouraged to take an active role in the management of the company's business by identifying challenges and implementing their own innovative plans. They are provided the resources necessary to meet their challenges, along with the authority to make decisions and follow through.

Efforts of Solar employees are rewarded through a generous profit-sharing plan and other incentives that encourage attention to quality. Solar's benefits package is considered highly competitive within the industry. A comprehensive Solar training program provides opportunities for employees to grow in both leadership and technical areas; higher education is encouraged through company reimbursement of tuition and books. Solar believes this level of commitment to its work force is valuable insurance for the company's future.

TOUCHING LIVES ACROSS THE GLOBE

Today, the big "made in San Diego" gas turbine engines turned out by Solar employees can be found on oil rigs in the North Sea, compressing natural gas as it comes from beneath the ocean, and pumping oil through pipelines in the Middle East, Texas, Brazil, Indonesia, and virtually anywhere else that oil and natural gas are produced.

Tourists arriving in Bermuda and Hawaii at the height of the season enjoy air conditioning and light produced by Solar-manufactured electricity "peaking" generator sets. Solar units produce steam and electrical power for processing kelp into valuable chemicals at San Diego's Kelco, Inc. and at industrial sites around the world. Nearly 100 Solar® gas turbines are compressing natural gas or generating electricity for pipelines in the Soviet Union, and many of the nation's telephone centers rely on Solar generators for emergency backup power.

Indeed, the company's employees and products contribute to the lives of people all over the world in many ways. From its beginnings in 1927, Solar Turbines Incorporated has continued to strive for innovation, adapting to—and creating—new technology and growing with San Diego.

Many components for Solar's gas turbines are produced at the Harbor Drive facility, which has been the company's headquarters since 1927.

GRAY, CARY, AMES & FRYE

INCE ITS FOUNDING IN 1927, GRAY, CARY, AMES & Frye has represented clients in every segment of the city's economy—ranging from aerospace to zoology. With a strong tradition of leadership in community affairs, the firm has long been considered a vital part of the community's economic and cultural infrastructure.

A FULL-SERVICE FIRM

Gray, Cary, Ames & Frye—a full-service law firm and the largest in San Diego—offers clients a wide spectrum of services. Its major areas of practice include litigation, employment law, general business, finance, tax, real estate, bankruptcy, and trusts and estates. The firm's 190 attorneys work at solving clients' problems through practice groups that cross industry and legal lines. These include such areas of law as environmental, high tech, international, biotech business, land development, product liability, construction, appellate, media, and family-owned businesses.

"Our clients enjoy both individual attention and the range of sophisticated legal resources that only a firm of our size can provide,"

Don Rushing became managing partner of Gray, Cary, Ames & Frye on January 1, 1992.

says Theodore Cranston, managing partner until January 1, 1992. "Our environmental group, for example, includes attorneys with legal skills in business, litigation, tax, real estate, and trusts and estates. Virtually every business or individual is touched by environmental issues."

Gray, Cary, Ames & Frye occupies seven floors of First Interstate Plaza in downtown San Diego and has additional offices in La Jolla, Escondido, and El Centro. At its headquarters, the firm maintains a 60,000-volume law library— the largest non-institutional library in the county—and a computerized legal research

> **"OUR CLIENTS ENJOY BOTH INDIVIDUAL ATTENTION AND THE RANGE OF SOPHISTICATED LEGAL RESOURCES THAT ONLY A FIRM OF OUR SIZE CAN PROVIDE," SAYS THEODORE CRANSTON. "OUR ENVIRONMENTAL GROUP, FOR EXAMPLE, INCLUDES ATTORNEYS WITH LEGAL SKILLS IN BUSINESS, LITIGATION, TAX, REAL ESTATE, AND TRUSTS AND ESTATES. VIRTUALLY EVERY BUSINESS OR INDIVIDUAL IS TOUCHED BY ENVIRONMENTAL ISSUES."**

system which is linked to government, regulatory, legal, and corporate data banks. Every attorney has a desktop computer that is part of a network linking all branches of the firm. In addition, attorneys are supported by a 260-person staff of administrators, legal analysts, paralegals, information system specialists, nurse consultants, and secretaries.

ORIGINS IN 1910

The firm was founded by Gordon L. Gray, who first came to San Diego from Chicago on legal business in 1907 and returned to open a law office in 1910. Gray initiated the firm's tradition of community service by quickly becoming involved in civic affairs, helping found the city's first Rotary Club. His first client was Colonel Ed Fletcher, a pioneer San Diegan responsible for development of much of the county.

In 1922, Gray hired Walter Ames, a Stanford graduate, and started another tradition that still exists: the firm takes on as associates graduates of the nation's top law schools, all of whom must be considered potential partners. In 1920, Gray hired the firm's first woman lawyer, Josephine

Ted Cranston served as the firm's managing partner until January 1, 1992.

Irving, setting a precedent of hiring women and minorities that remains in place today.

Ames quickly became a prominent figure in San Diego, helping organize the historic California Pacific International Exposition, which ultimately was responsible for developing Balboa Park—one of the city's crown jewels. Ames conceived, organized, and led construction of the nationally-recognized Timken Art Museum in Balboa Park. He also assisted in founding the San Diego Taxpayers Association and San Diegans, Inc., both of which are now major downtown leadership groups.

In 1925, Gray hired J.G. Driscoll, another Stanford graduate. Superior Court Judge William P. Cary joined the firm in 1926. A year later, the new partnership of Gray, Cary, Ames & Driscoll was introduced to the community. The last of the founding partners—Frank Frye, a graduate of Stanford University and Harvard Law School—joined the firm in 1934.

When Driscoll left to establish his own practice in 1951, Frye was added to the firm name which became Gray, Cary, Ames & Frye. It hasn't changed since.

INVOLVED IN COMMUNITY AFFAIRS

From the time of the firm's founding, its lawyers have played an important role in community affairs—organizing, shaping, and encouraging civic, cultural, business, and government endeavors.

For over 60 years Gray, Cary, Ames & Frye attorneys have played roles in almost every cultural, business, social, and nonprofit philanthropic organization in the county. Among these are policy-making, director, or advisory roles at the Old Globe Theatre, San Diego Symphony, San Diego Opera, area universities, museums, art groups, hospitals, health organizations, and libraries. The firm's roster of attorney members in business circles includes membership and leadership positions in area chambers of commerce, economic development agencies, transborder organizations, and international trade groups.

"Our goal is to have every one of our lawyers involved in some community activity, whether it be as a church group or local PTA member or as the head of the Chamber," says Cranston. "It's a cliche to say we believe in giving back to the community, but it's also the truth."

The firm maintains its ongoing relationship with the community and its clients by publishing eight newsletters and a general quarterly publication. With circulations ranging from 600 to 14,000 copies, the aim of the publications is to keep everyone abreast of legal developments and trends in business and industry, as well as to educate clients on potential strategic problems and solutions. The firm also holds about 30 seminars annually for discussion of more immediate topics.

"We are in touch with the latest developments in the business community and the law," says Don Rushing, current managing partner. "Thus, we are able to anticipate our clients' legal needs. We often suggest preventative steps that help avert a potential crisis."

The firm is particularly proud of the thousands of hours of legal representation donated each year as part of its pro bono program. In addition, its lawyers are held in such regard by the legal community that they are often selected as mediators, arbitrators, and private judges to settle disputes. With such strong community ties and established legal expertise, Gray, Cary, Ames & Frye plans to continue to play a central role in the future development of San Diego.

> "WE ARE IN TOUCH WITH THE LATEST DEVELOPMENTS IN THE BUSINESS COMMUNITY AND THE LAW," SAYS DON RUSHING, CURRENT MANAGING PARTNER. "THUS, WE ARE ABLE TO ANTICIPATE OUR CLIENTS' LEGAL NEEDS. WE OFTEN SUGGEST PREVENTATIVE STEPS THAT HELP AVERT A POTENTIAL CRISIS."

The founders of the firm made significant contributions to the community of San Diego. FROM LEFT: Gordon Gray, W.P. Cary, Walter Ames, and Frank Frye.

SHEPPARD, MULLIN, RICHTER & HAMPTON

N THE ECONOMIC HARD TIMES OF THE 1930S, hordes of creative, hardworking Americans moved westward in hopes of finding jobs—a population shift that initiated California's transformation into a modern economic giant. Simultaneously, new laws passed in response to the Great Depression forever reshaped the U.S. financial industry and created new challenges and opportunities for the fledgling law firm of Sheppard, Mullin, Richter & Hampton.

GROWING WITH CALIFORNIA

The history of the firm, founded in 1927, parallels the phenomenal growth of California. As the state economy expanded, Sheppard, Mullin, Richter & Hampton grew into one of California's premier legal practices, specializing in banking and finance law.

During the Depression, the firm addressed revolutionary new banking laws by giving counsel and anticipating and solving problems for clients. Sheppard, Mullin, Richter & Hampton also helped solidify operating policies for the state's major banking and finance institutions, many of whom remain clients of the firm today. For example, George Richter Jr., a senior partner in the firm, helped draft California's commercial code, saw it passed into law, and then became its chief interpreter. His commitment to the firm's role as a statewide leader in business law remains strong today.

"That's still a strategic goal," says Victor A. Vilaplana, administrative partner, "only now it applies to every field of law."

With 240 lawyers in four California cities, Sheppard, Mullin, Richter & Hampton continues to broaden its areas of legal expertise. Long known as one of the state's top full-service legal practices, the firm maintains recognized specialties in banking, litigation, corporate and tax law, real estate, labor law, and estate planning. Other practice groups within the firm include environmental, white collar crime, and international law.

Since the 1930s, Sheppard, Mullin, Richter & Hampton has helped shape the labor policies of many of the state's top employers. Likewise, the firm has guided and counseled major California builders and developers through economic ups and downs and has handled some of the toughest business battles in courtrooms throughout the state.

> "AT THE RISK OF BEING IMMODEST," SAYS SAN DIEGO PARTNER CHRISTOPHER B. NEILS, "OUR CONSTANT BUSINESS GOAL IS TO BE ON EVERYONE'S SHORT LIST OF THE TOP THREE TO FIVE LAW FIRMS IN THE STATE. AND THAT MEANS UTILIZING TALENT AND RESOURCES TO GIVE QUALITY ADVICE AND SERVICE ON A TIMELY BASIS AT A FAIR PRICE."

"At the risk of being immodest," says San Diego partner Christopher B. Neils, "our constant business goal is to be on everyone's short list of the top three to five law firms in the state. And that means utilizing talent and resources to give quality advice and service on a timely basis at a fair price."

SERVING SAN DIEGO SINCE 1986

The firm was founded in Los Angeles in 1927 by William C. Mathes, Raymond L. Haight, and James C. Sheppard. Over the years, the partnership has evolved into Sheppard, Mullin, Richter & Hampton. Today, the firm maintains offices in Los Angeles, San Diego, San Francisco, and Newport Beach.

After the San Diego location opened on March 1, 1986, it quickly became a significant force in the legal community. To complement its enormous resources and historic expertise, the firm set out to create a "homegrown" practice. The five attorneys who established the San Diego office—including Vilaplana and Neils—were partners and department heads recruited from two of the city's top law firms. Today, over 30 attorneys at Sheppard,

San Diego attorneys Christopher B. Neils, James J. Mittermiller, and Laura S. Taylor on the stairway between the 18th and 19th floors of the firm's offices at 501 West Broadway.

Mullin, Richter & Hampton in San Diego serve a deep and diverse client base.

From the new waterfront Koll Center on West Broadway, the firm represents clients ranging from multinational banks and corporations to local businesses, from large real estate developers to a couple buying their first home, from multiple parties in complex federal litigation to neighborhood disputes, from national department store chains to local retailers, from multistate construction companies to local contractors. Beyond its expertise in the financial field, Sheppard, Mullin, Richter & Hampton serves international firms and clients in numerous industries, including venture capital, aerospace, aircraft, oil and gas, retailing, insurance, and high tech research and manufacturing.

Like most large law firms, Sheppard, Mullin, Richter & Hampton maintains a traditional in-house law library. But its attorneys also use a state-of-the-art computerized database library, including access to such enormous information banks as LEXIS and Westlaw. All four California offices are linked through the firm's computer network. Each attorney's office is wired for a desktop terminal, and an increasing number of attorneys have and use them.

Pro Bono and Community Service

Demonstrating a strong commitment to the community, many members of the San Diego office are leaders in business, cultural, and civic activities, supporting such organizations as the Chamber of Commerce, YMCA, Economic Education Foundation, La Jolla Art Museum, the San Diego Zoo, Aerospace Museum, and the Economic Development Corporation. A believer in and supporter of equal opportunity, the firm is a participant in the California Minority Counsel Program and has both partners and associates from minority ethnic groups.

Likewise, Sheppard, Mullin, Richter & Hampton has a long tradition of providing legal service to the community's needy without charge. The firm's official policy is to "encourage and facilitate pro bono activities." To that end, Sheppard, Mullin, Richter & Hampton established a Committee on Legal Services comprised of partners and associates from all four offices. The firm's pro bono work has included political asylum cases, representation of abused and battered women, preservation of historical landmarks, and representation of indigents in a variety of litigation matters. The firm was named "Pro Bono Firm of the Year" for both 1989 and 1990 in San Diego and received a similar honor in 1990 from the California State Bar Association.

From its beginnings during the Great Depression, the firm has maintained a strong commitment to its home state of California. Through the years, its areas of expertise have extended far beyond the original concentration on banking and finance law. As San Diego emerges as a major economic center on the West Coast and beyond, Sheppard, Mullin, Richter & Hampton is well prepared to meet the increasingly complex and diverse legal needs of the community.

SAN DIEGO CONVENTION AND VISITORS BUREAU

RGANIZED EFFORTS TO ATTRACT VISITORS TO SAN Diego have long been a major element of public policy of both the metropolitan area's leadership structure and its governments. And economic support by the public has been its backbone.

As far back as 1919, the community recognized that income from visitors, whether they be family day-trippers, new residents, or five-day convention-eers, meant new dollars for the community. Today, visitors constitute the area's third largest job-creating, income-producing industry, after manufacturing and the federal government.

Visitor attraction programs are based on the philosophy that there are many reasons to visit San Diego in addition to its semi-tropical climate.

Nature's sandy beaches, oceanfront parks, and pine mountain recreation areas under mild sunshine and cool breezes are where it all begins, of course.

But there are such manmade attractions as a trolley ride to Mexico, offshore sailing, Charger football games, and a visit to Old Town, where the Spanish padres erected the first mission and thus founded what later became California.

In addition, San Diego offers Sea World, the Zoo, major league Padres baseball, the Space Theater, deep sea fishing, acres of museums in Balboa Park, and two legitimate theaters, where Broadway plays are born. Visitors can take a waterfront stroll to Sea Port Village and the ancient sailing ship, the Star of India. Along the city's waterfront, tourists can also see the tuna fleet docks, where city-block-size nets are repaired; the terminal, where cruise ships dock; and perhaps a sailboat on a tuning run for an America's Cup race.

Convention delegates se-lect a dining spot with the help of knowledge-able personnel at the ConVis restaurant booth at the Convention Center.

A PRIVATE, NONPROFIT ORGANIZATION

Charged with spreading the word about all this—and representing an industry that brings in almost $3.5 billion a year in new money—is the San Diego Convention and Visitors Bureau.

ConVis, as it's known informally, is a private, nonprofit organization supported by taxes, contribu-tions, and dues from member business firms. Its goal is to build a better community through the visitor industry, marketing the county as a vacation destina-tion and convention site.

Over the years, ConVis has evolved from the organization formed in 1919 by real estate man O.W. Cotton. Cotton's San Diego-California Club had as its original goal to persuade Americans to move to San Diego, which was in a serious economic slump. Toward that objective, the community raised $150,000—an enormous sum for a city of 85,000 in an economically tight wartime era.

The advertising and promotion campaign was successful beyond Cotton's dreams. Downtown growth began, a construction boom followed, and new homes were sold. Ultimately, the innovative effort created a pattern for success that has since been adopted by tourist bureaus around the world.

The message: Correctly publicize your assets, and success will follow.

Today, the Convention and Visitors Bureau re-ceives 84 percent of its operating funds, primarily generated by hotel room taxes, from the government. The remainder comes from membership dues and contributions.

Its 75 employees are involved in various depart-ments, including visitor services, research, convention sales, hospitality training programs, convention serv-ices, public relations, membership sales, marketing, and travel industry sales.

Local residents and out-of-town visitors are drawn to events in San Diego's new Convention Center. (Photo: West Coast Projections, Inc.)

A MONUMENT TO COMMUNITY SUPPORT

Strong community support for facilities to accommo-date groups of visitors did not always exist. In fact, San Diegans rejected the concept of a tax supported convention center at 14 elections between World War II and 1964, when the downtown Convention and Performing Arts Center was finally opened.

Today, visitor groups meet in a new 760,000-square-foot waterfront convention complex opened in 1990, that is a monument to community support. The facility was built by the San Diego Port District without the use of tax funds. Operated by the city of San Diego, the center is enjoying record-breaking business thanks to the efforts of the ConVis sales team and the convention center teams. From the day it opened, plans were being made to double its size.

"The new convention center is now strongly supported by the many hotels built during the recent six-year hotel construction boom," says ConVis president Reint Reinders. "Strategically, we now are focusing on the convention center expansion, a new international airport, and better international air service."

1930-1969

1934

HOMEFED BANK, FSB

1936

DEL MAR FAIRGROUNDS

1945

HARTSON MEDICAL SERVICES

1946

SHARP HEALTHCARE

1960

THE SALK INSTITUTE FOR BIOLOGICAL STUDIES

1965

SAN DIEGO ECONOMIC DEVELOPMENT CORPORATION

1968

IVAC CORPORATION

SINCE 1936, THE DEL MAR FAIRGROUNDS HAS provided a major recreation and entertainment venue for Southern Californians. All the things that say "California" to the rest of the world—beaches, movie star glamour, horse racing, sports, entertainment, and sunshine—can be found at the oceanfront facility.

Covering over 350 acres, the fairgrounds annually hosts numerous community, agricultural, social, and trade events, including national horse shows and dog shows, regional auto racing, ethnic festivals, and home shows. But the two premier events that have been held each summer at the fairgrounds since the 1930s are the Del Mar Fair and the thoroughbred race meet. In 1987, satellite wagering on races throughout Southern California became a year-round activity, drawing patrons to the grounds even when live racing is not scheduled.

SINCE THE 1930S, THE TWO PREMIER EVENTS THAT HAVE BEEN HELD EACH SUMMER AT THE FAIRGROUNDS ARE THE DEL MAR FAIR AND THE THOROUGHBRED RACE MEET.

OVER 1 MILLION FAIRGROUNDS VISITORS

The Del Mar Fair is the second largest agricultural fair in California and the 13th largest in North America based on attendance during its 20-day run from mid-June through the Fourth of July holiday. The fair offers entertainment by national artists and community groups, as well as opportunities for residents and visitors to San Diego County to learn about local agriculture.

More than 1 million visitors come each year to see the award-winning flower and garden show, numerous action-packed arena events, a junior livestock auction, international photography, and thousands of exhibits provided by children, adults, and seniors from the community. Popular attractions include hundreds of fair and food concessions, a safe, clean carnival and midway, and daily grandstand shows featuring top entertainers.

For nearly 50 years, the Del Mar Fairgrounds has hosted the annual Del Mar National Horse Show with champion horse and rider teams from throughout the western United States. In 1991, a new $5.4 million equestrian facility was built to enhance the

Riders of all ages compete in the Del Mar National Horse Show during its two-week run in May at the Del Mar Fairgrounds. (Photo: 22nd District Agricultural Association)

enjoyment of Southern California horse enthusiasts. With permanent seating for 4,000, an expansive arena floor, and state-of-the-art sound and lighting, the arena features an equestrian event nearly every weekend such as breed shows, rodeo competitions, and polo matches.

For the first time on the West Coast and only the third time in the United States, the world championship of show jumping, the Volvo World Cup, will come to the fairgrounds in 1992. The event features nearly 100 horse and rider teams from throughout the world competing for the coveted title. Five days of spectacular horsemanship will dominate the arena for international spectators.

Clearly, horses are an important part of life throughout the area. Despite rapid urbanization, San Diego County continues to have the largest equine population per capita of any county in the nation, according to Department of Agriculture reports. Horses—primarily racing thoroughbreds—have been steady visitors to the Del Mar Fairgrounds through the years. The fairgrounds also serves as the sales headquarters of the California Thoroughbred Breeders' Association, offering auctions of some of the best young racing stock in the state four times each year.

A MAJOR RENOVATION PLAN

The fairgrounds and its facilities are owned and managed by the 22nd District Agricultural Association, a state agency dedicated to producing the fair and providing other annual and recreational outlets for local residents. Appointed by the governor, the

One of the most popular exhibits at the Del Mar Fair is its Flower and Garden Show, which showcases San Diego County's finest displays of cut flowers and landscape design. (Photo: 22nd District Agricultural Association)

District Board of Directors is charged with assisting and encouraging agricultural education.

Through resources generated on the fairgrounds, the District has begun a major renovation plan to bring the grounds into the 21st century. Spanish-style architecture used in the original fairgrounds design is replicated throughout the new construction, recalling the architectural heritage of the Spanish missions.

In addition to the $5.4 million horse arena, a $15 million satellite wagering facility was constructed in 1991. It offers a sophisticated environment for horse racing enthusiasts to wager on thoroughbred, harness, and quarter horse meets through simultaneous broadcasting from other tracks in California and across the nation. Satellite wagering is open year-round except during the Del Mar race meet.

An exciting $80 million grandstand reconstruction project includes a new 15,000-seat grandstand (formerly 9,500 seats) for racing and concert entertainment, a new racetrack administration/operations building and receiving barn, and a replacement exhibit building adjacent to the new grandstand. Numerous meeting rooms, restaurants, outdoor race viewing areas, and exhibit and concession space for fair time will round out the abundance of new amenities.

Scheduled for completion in 1994, the grandstand construction will take place in three 10-month phases, from September through June in 1991, 1992, and 1993. The first phase included the demolition of the western two-thirds of the grandstand and the three adjacent exhibit buildings. Prior to the start of the 1992 fair and racing season, partial occupancy of the western portion of the new facility is expected.

Nightly concerts at the Del Mar Fair feature top-name recording artists. BELOW: Melissa Manchester entertains at the 1991 Del Mar Fair. (Photo: 22nd District Agricultural Association)

"WHERE THE TURF MEETS THE SURF"

The fairgrounds is also the home of the Del Mar Thoroughbred Club and its annual racing meet, currently the most successful in the country. The thoroughbred racing season is operated by Del Mar Thoroughbred Club on a lease arrangement with the 22nd District as agent of the State of California. The track, only a chip shot from the blue Pacific, presents sleek thoroughbreds in action from late July through mid-September.

Singer Bing Crosby, one of the founders of racing at Del Mar, did much to popularize the new track when he crooned its theme, "Where the Turf Meets the Surf." The song is still played daily before the first race and after the last race during the 43-day summer session.

Horses—primarily racing thoroughbreds—have been steady visitors to the Del Mar Fairgrounds through the years. (Photo: Del Mar Thoroughbred Club)

The fairgrounds is the home of the Del Mar Thoroughbred Club and its annual racing meet, currently the most successful in the country. (Photo: Venture Inc.)

Horse racing at Del Mar has attracted countless Hollywood celebrities since opening day on July 3, 1937, when Crosby cut the ribbon to admit the first patron. Archives of the Thoroughbred Club are filled with photos of movie greats and notables such as Dick Powell, Barbara Stanwyck, J. Edgar Hoover, Jackie Cooper, Lucille Ball, Desi Arnaz, Betty Grable, Harry James, Edward G. Robinson, Joe Frisco, Red Skelton, Jimmy Durante, and Hoagie Carmichael. All of the big-name jockeys have made their mark at

HORSE RACING AT DEL MAR HAS ATTRACTED COUNTLESS HOLLYWOOD CELEBRITIES SINCE OPENING DAY ON JULY 3, 1937, WHEN BING CROSBY CUT THE RIBBON TO ADMIT THE FIRST PATRON.

Del Mar, including Bill Shoemaker and John Longden, who set world records for winners at the seaside track. Equine champions from Seabiscuit to Native Diver to Ferdinand have thrilled crowds over the years.

Since 1970, the track has been operated by the Del Mar Thoroughbred Club, which has fostered its growth from a cozy, resort track to the leading thoroughbred meeting in North America. In 1991, Del Mar and its satellites averaged more than $7.8 million in daily average parimutuel handle and more than 37,000 in daily average attendance. Today, thanks in part to Crosby's vision and Del Mar's current success, the California horse industry contributes $2 billion a year to the state's economy.

Throughout its history, millions of people have enjoyed the activities of the Del Mar Fairgrounds, and many historical milestones can be claimed at this famous oceanfront facility. The ongoing annual fair and live race meet continue to provide entertainment, while new activities join the calendar of events, bringing patrons back time and time again to the beautiful Southern California site.

The architectural heritage of the Spanish missions, which inspired the original fairgrounds design (below), is maintained throughout the new construction at Del Mar. (Photo: Venture Inc.)

HomeFed Bank, FSB

T WAS 1934, AND THE ENTIRE NATION WAS GRIPPED by the Depression. Unemployment was rampant, government food lines were long, and businesses closed almost daily. The U.S. economy was in the worst shape since the decade following the Civil War.

It was hardly the most auspicious time to start a savings institution, particularly one with a goal of financing the construction of new homes.

But the community needed a credible financing source at a time when banks were failing. And so, Home Federal Savings and Loan (now HomeFed Bank, FSB) was born. It was to be a secure place where people could earn interest on their savings. Their money would in turn be loaned to fellow depositors to build homes.

HomeFed was founded during the Depression as a secure place where people could earn interest on their savings.

$2,000 of his own savings, Fletcher obtained a savings and loan charter on August 27, 1934. For some time, he remained the bank's sole employee, working at a borrowed desk in a corner of his father's office.

It was Charles Fletcher who selected the name "Home" for the new institution. "I always liked that word," he said. "I love my home, and the articles by which all federal savings and loans are created use the words 'home ownership' and 'thrift.' I believe that a home is one of the foundations of our liberty."

ABOVE: Charles K. Fletcher, founder of HomeFed Bank. ABOVE RIGHT: Kim Fletcher, chairman of the board and son of the founder.

Founded by the Fletcher Family

HomeFed Bank was founded by the Fletcher family, a San Diego dynasty that has played a leadership role throughout the community since shortly after the turn of the century. Over the years, the influence of the Fletchers has impacted suburban and city development, the law, community resources such as water, libraries, schools, and highways, and wide-ranging cultural activities.

Ed Fletcher, father of HomeFed's founder, is generally remembered by historians as one of several farsighted individuals responsible for developing San Diego. By creating a series of holding reservoirs, including Cuyamaca, Henshaw, and Hodges, Fletcher built a water distribution system for what was then a small town with a barren desert-like climate. He was also responsible for initiating and building such communities as Fletcher Hills, Mount Helix, Pine Hills, and Del Mar.

His son, Charles K. Fletcher, started HomeFed more than half a century ago with $7,500 in pledges from 50 San Diegans. With these slips of paper and

The Seventh Largest U.S. Thrift

Headquartered in San Diego, HomeFed has become one of the city's major financial institutions with more than 200 branch offices and 3,200 employees throughout California. Its $14 billion in assets and $10 billion in deposits make the thrift the seventh largest in the United States.

A major consumer bank and real estate lender, HomeFed is today led by Kim Fletcher, the son of founder Charles Fletcher. Having joined the firm in 1950 after graduating from Stanford, Kim became president of the bank on its 30th anniversary. Like his father and grandfather, Kim has been a major player in community affairs, ranging from economic to political. Since his retirement as CEO in 1990, Kim has continued to play an active role as chairman of the board. Thomas J. Wageman now serves as the company's president and chief executive.

From its humble beginnings in 1934 as a tiny mutual savings organization with one employee to its modern incarnation as the seventh largest savings institution in the country, HomeFed has remained a valuable economic resource for all of its customers.

Thomas J. Wageman, Home Fed's president and CEO.

SHARP HEALTHCARE

S HARP HEALTHCARE IS SAN DIEGO'S MOST COMPRE- hensive health care delivery system. A homegrown institution founded almost half a century ago by a group of community leaders, it operates five major hospitals, 13 clinics, five nursing centers, and a wide variety of related facilities.

SETTING HEALTH CARE STANDARDS

Despite significant growth, Sharp adheres to the goal established by its founders in 1946: to provide quality care and services that set commu- nity standards. Today, the organization sees this as its long-range mission and as an explanation of how such a large institution continues to function so well.

Sharp performed the com- munity's first open heart sur- gery several years after its original hospital opened in 1955. Sharp also founded the county's first health care facility exclusively for women, opened the first hospital-based alcohol and drug treatment center, performed the area's first heart transplant, and initiated the first use of the artificial heart on the West Coast. In 1990, Sharp began kidney and lung transplantation.

One of every five babies born in San Diego is delivered at Sharp. With patients coming from four adjacent counties, Sharp performs more open heart surgeries than any other health care system in the region. Several of the organization's specialty cen- ters—cardiac, women's care, rehabilitation, and sub- stance abuse—are considered regional medical re- sources. Its work force, totaling over 9,500 employees, is one of the largest in the area. More than 2,000 physicians affiliated with Sharp provide services in virtually all medical and surgical specialties.

Sharp HealthCare, a not-for-profit organization, operates Sharp Memorial Hospital in Kearny Mesa with 581 licensed beds. Its other hospitals, networked throughout the county, include Grossmont Hospital in La Mesa with 464 beds, Sharp Cabrillo Hospital with 250 beds, Community Hospital in Chula Vista with 236 beds, and Sharp HealthCare Murrieta in Riverside County with 49 beds.

The organization also operates eight Sharp Rees- Stealy Medical Centers, two clinics exclusively for seniors, and five convalescent hospitals: Sharp Knoll- wood, Sharp Meadowlark, Sharp HealthCare Murri- eta, Sharp Cabrillo, and Birch-Patrick.

> **"SHARP IS UNQUESTIONABLY WOVEN INTO THE FABRIC OF SAN DIEGO," SAYS JAMES C. HAUGH, CHAIRMAN OF THE BOARD. "BECAUSE OF THIS AND THE BOARD'S PROGRESSIVE THINKING AND UNWAVERING COMMITMENT, SHARP HAS BEEN PROPELLED TO THE FOREFRONT OF HEALTH CARE."**

FOUNDED ON COMMUNITY GENEROSITY

Sharp began in the mid-1940s after a group of community leaders studied local health care demands and concluded that San Diego needed a new hospital. In 1946, a citizens' group organized the San Diego Hospital Association and began making plans and raising funds.

Thomas Sharp, a rancher and radio communications pi- oneer, contributed $500,000 in memory of his son, Air Force Lieutenant Donald N. Sharp, a native San Diegan who died in World War II. After philanthropist Phillip Gildred Sr. donated the site for a hospital in Kearny Mesa, members of the community opened their pocketbooks, do- nating generously to the ven- ture. In April 1955, the new Donald N. Sharp Memorial Community Hospital finally opened its doors. As the first new hospital built in the community in 27 years, it immediately relieved a critical shortage of medical and surgical beds.

The community leaders who founded the hospital remained involved in its operation, serving as the first board of directors. Along with other dedicated San Diegans, they have maintained their initial commit- ment over the years, ensuring that Sharp remains a locally-controlled organization that understands the community's ever-increasing need for quality health care services. The community, in turn, supports the organization with contributions to the foundations at Sharp and Grossmont hospitals.

"Sharp is unquestionably woven into the fabric of San Diego," says James C. Haugh, chairman of the board. "Because of this and the board's progressive thinking and unwavering commitment, Sharp has been propelled to the forefront of health care."

EXPANDING TO MEET COMMUNITY NEEDS

As community needs have changed over the years, Sharp has expanded to meet them, carefully acquiring other hospitals, sophisticated medical equipment, outpatient clinics, and specialty facilities. "The oppor- tunity to improve the quality of care or the scope of health care services for San Diego has been the moving force for the board in making each of these major growth decisions," says Peter K. Ellsworth, president and chief executive officer.

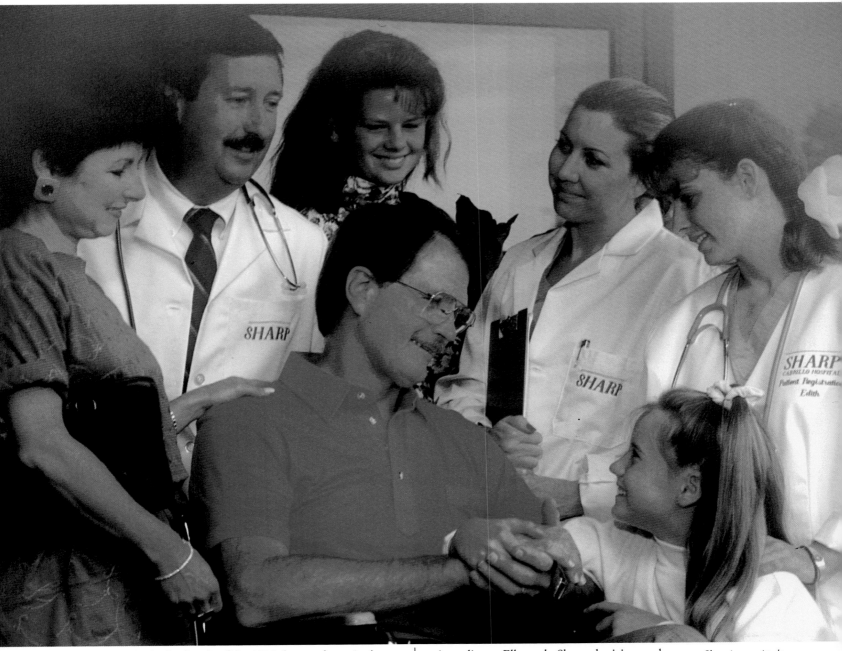

As the decade of the 1980s began, the nation's health care industry changed drastically as it simultaneously faced government deregulation and an increase in regulations aimed at reducing costs. Sharp has met those challenges head-on by placing greater emphasis on ambulatory care, in-home treatment, patient education, and outpatient and emergency care.

According to Ellsworth, Sharp physicians and support staff have two major roles—caring for people and teaching them to care for themselves. "By fulfilling both of these roles in a variety of settings and locations," he explains, "Sharp stands out as a health care leader. We believe that only through such a systematic approach of preventive medicine and quality care can we effectively address the economic and health care issues of the future."

Sharp is committed to improving the health of the community through its conveniently located facilities and services. With a staff of over 9,500 employees and a network of 2,000 affiliated physicians, Sharp is caring in so many ways.

HARTSON MEDICAL SERVICES

ARTSON MEDICAL SERVICES, HEADQUARTERED IN San Diego, is the largest private emergency medical care and transportation company in the nation. Founded shortly after World War II, Hartson—and its parent company MedTrans—has served San Diego since 1945.

OFFERING THE BEST IN EMERGENCY MEDICAL CARE

Providing on-the-scene medical care, as well as transportation from accidents, fires, aircraft crashes, and other emergency situations, the firm today provides paramedic service for the city of San Diego and 11 suburban communities: Rancho Santa Fe, Encinitas, Solana Beach, La Mesa, Lemon Grove, Spring Valley, Imperial Beach, National City, Chula Vista, San Marcos, and Del Mar. Hartson's fleet of 100 ambulances has become a familiar sight on San Diego streets. Every year, its 175 jump-suited paramedics transport more than 50,000 patients.

In addition to quick-response, advanced life support services, Hartson operates an equally large basic life support department that responds to non-emergency calls throughout San Diego County. With a staff of 150 emergency medical technicians (EMTs), Hartson transports patients to and from hospitals, specialty medical facilities, convalescent and nursing centers, and patients' homes.

Hartson Medical Services today provides paramedic service for the city of San Diego and 11 suburban communities.

VARIOUS GOVERNMENT AGENCIES HAVE CALLED UPON HARTSON FOR ASSISTANCE IN SETTING CRITERIA FOR EMERGENCY MEDICAL ORGANIZATIONS.

Hartson also operates four critical care vehicles that transport neonatal, pediatric, and critically ill patients throughout several counties. In addition to traditional paramedic services, the specially-equipped mobile intensive care units are rolling emergency rooms staffed by registered nurses trained as mobile intensive care transport supervisors.

Thanks to its success in the emergency medical care industry, Hartson has become the "how to" consultant to emergency care providers nationwide. In fact, various government agencies have called upon the firm for assistance in setting criteria for emergency medical organizations, including critical requirements for vehicles, incident response times, and personnel training.

EXPANSION FROM A SAN DIEGO BASE

Hartson's gradual expansion throughout the West into such areas as Las Vegas, Seattle, Fort Worth, Santa Ana, Long Beach, and San Mateo and Orange counties has motivated the company to tailor its operations to the varying needs of the cities it serves. In answer to its own growth and the increased diversity within its corporate structure, Hartson created MedTrans. Serving as Hartson's parent company, MedTrans provides expert technical support for the various subsidiary firms as well, including Mercy Medical Services, Inc. in Las Vegas; Texas Lifeline Corporation, operating as MedStar in Fort Worth; American MedTech in Seattle; BayStar Medical Services in San Mateo County, California; and Superior Ambulance Service in Santa Ana, Long Beach, and Orange County, California.

Based in San Diego, Hartson and the other subsidiaries of MedTrans are owned by Thomas W. Morgan and Glen R. Roberts. The local firm's 500 employees, with 1,000 more in its other operations, range from paramedics and EMTs to registered nurses, physicians, communications experts, computer technicians, clerks, billing specialists, and a vehicle maintenance staff.

Over the years, Hartson has continually set standards for professional operation throughout the emergency medical care industry. "We believe we set the standards," says Roberts, "and our strategic growth philosophy is based on that principle."

"We will continue to grow and expand," adds Morgan, "but at a rate commensurate with quality care and preservation of our standards."

HE SALK INSTITUTE FOR BIOLOGICAL STUDIES manifests both architectural and scientific creativity. Overlooking the Pacific Ocean from atop a cliff in La Jolla, the Institute is a vision made real, the vision of a man who erased the world's fear of a deadly disease.

Dr. Jonas Salk's inspiration was to create an environment that encourages creativity in fundamental research at the frontiers of the biological sciences. Today, the Salk Institute is one of the world's largest independent facilities for biomedical research. The common goal of its scientists is to gain fundamental knowledge of vital biological operations, including those of the brain, the immune system, the genes, and the AIDS virus. Such knowledge is essential to the success of efforts to conquer the myriad diseases that burden human lives.

"WHEREVER THEIR RESEARCH LEADS THEM, THE SCIENTISTS MAY PURSUE," NOTES NOBEL LAUREATE DR. RENATO DULBECCO, THE INSTITUTE'S CURRENT PRESIDENT.

The research papers published by Salk scientists are among the most frequently cited in the scientific world. Many of the faculty's 47 members are recognized internationally as leaders in their fields. Three faculty members are Nobel laureates, and six are members of the National Academy of Sciences.

A CREATIVE RESEARCH ENVIRONMENT
Founded in 1960 with major funding from the March of Dimes, the Salk Institute is a private research facility with few of the constraints of more traditional institutions. It allows its scientists the freedom to explore exciting new ideas as they arise. "Wherever their research leads them, the scientists may pursue," notes Nobel laureate Dr. Renato Dulbecco, the Institute's current president.

"I wanted to establish a creative environment, a crucible for creativity," Salk wrote recently. "What would happen, I asked myself, if biologists, on the verge of discovering the secrets of life and of evolution, could work together in an environment that would prompt them to consider the wider implications of their discoveries for the future?"

"It is truly a special place to do science," adds Dr. Inder Verma, chairman of the faculty. "We can go wherever our inspiration takes us."

As a result, research at the Salk Institute has contributed to the solution of many health problems, including cancer, birth defects, growth deficiencies, viral infections, and memory loss.

Studies at the Salk Institute fall into six broad domains: brain research, cancer, molecular medicine, human heredity, plant biology, and AIDS. Scientists from diverse backgrounds pursue the molecular organization of cells, the control of gene activity, the

formation of the brain, mental retardation, and a host of other biological puzzles. All are searching for keys to the improvement of human well-being.

"AN ACROPOLIS OF SCIENCE"
The Institute's austere campus of concrete, marble, and teak buildings is known worldwide for its extraordinary architecture. It was created by famed architect-philosopher Louis Kahn, who worked with Salk to achieve a serene, collegial environment that has subsequently been termed "an acropolis of science."

"Salk's goal of creating a campus crucible for creativity," said Kahn, "really electrified me; the belief that makes a painter paint must be constantly felt by the scientist so that he never forgets in his measurable work that the unmeasurable desires somehow have come together."

With an annual budget of $37 million, the Institute has a total staff of more than 500 members. Over 200 of them are doctoral level scientists. Its board of trustees consists of national and world leaders in the fields of art, science, business, and industry.

The Salk apothegm, "Basic Research—Key to Health," truly represents the philosophy that prevails on the campus. One researcher recently predicted that the molecular biology research performed at Salk will one day put gene therapy into the physician's black bag as an approach to disease. Undoubtedly, this forward-looking attitude will continue to fuel the Institute's pursuit of knowledge to help conquer disease in the decades ahead.

The Institute's austere campus of concrete, marble, and teak buildings is known worldwide for its extraordinary architecture created by famed architect-philosopher Louis Kahn.

OR ALMOST A DECADE, THE ECONOMY OF THE San Diego region has set new growth records year after year. As the 1990s began, the gross regional product was an impressive $51 billion, which would rank San Diego 35th in the world if the county were a nation. Long ago, such numbers laid to rest San Diego's reputation as merely a Navy town or a beach resort with a good zoo.

But the numbers also point to the success of the San Diego Economic Development Corporation. Created in 1965, its purpose was to seek diversity and stabilize the economy of a city that was then known, primarily because of fluctuations in military spending, as a boom and bust town. Now more than 25 years old, EDC is a private, nonprofit corporation run by San Diego's leading business executives with major funding support from the city, the port district, and the county, as well as membership dues from the business community.

"We are always asked by out-of-state corporate officials whether San Diego is pro business and whether business is supported by the public sector," says Daniel O. Pegg, EDC president, "and the answer is an obvious 'yes,' which is substantiated by our own funding sources."

ASSISTING BUSINESS AND INDUSTRY

EDC's goal is simply to assist in the expansion and growth of existing industry and attract new business and industry to the region. But the organization's staff of employees—skilled in business development, research, and marketing—does much more than assist specific companies. EDC often takes leadership roles on broad public policy issues helpful to business in general.

"For a metropolitan area the size of San Diego, direct and indirect economic impacts of airport activity could generate as much as $844 billion in annual benefits by 2005," says Richard A. Cramer, EDC chairman, "to say nothing about the benefits of doing business with Pacific Rim countries."

Geographically, San Diego is in a marvelous position to take advantage of developing markets in Pacific Rim countries. Of equal importance to the region's economy is the elimination of most trade barriers between Mexico, Canada, and the United States.

"Such trade will play a crucial role in the economic future of San Diego," says Pegg. "By the year 2000, 25 percent of California's revenues will be generated by international trade related activities."

With an annual budget of roughly $1 million, EDC underwrites a wide variety of activities on behalf of business, including major programs to aid local business expansion. The organization also promotes San Diego to outside industries, emphasizing its accessibility by sea, air, or land, a big labor pool, a moderate climate, academic and high-end support, a huge consumer market, and cultural diversity.

Throughout its history, EDC's efforts have helped San Diego achieve stability through economic diversity. Today, the region's manufacturing, biotechnology, retail-wholesale, and high technology industries complement tourism and military spending to create a generally balanced economy. With continued support from EDC, San Diego is sure to remain a major contributor to the financial good health of Southern California.

The San Diego Economic Development Corporation strives to assist in the expansion and growth of existing industry and to attract new business and industry to the region. (Photo: San Diego Union)

IVAC CORPORATION

MEDICAL DEVICE COMPANY, IVAC CORPORATION IS dedicated to setting new standards of health care through differential products which meet customer needs, excellence in customer relationships, superior quality, continuous improvement, and the total involvement of every employee. As a consistent performer in the medical segment of San Diego's economy, IVAC enjoys a unique symbiotic relationship with the community's universities, teaching hospitals, and biotechnology industries.

A HISTORY OF INNOVATION AND QUALITY

IVAC was founded in San Diego in 1968 by a team of engineers who designed and built an instrument to control the flow of fluid given to patients intravenously. This innovative instrument was designed to sound an alarm when the bottle was empty. IVAC also developed the first electronic, digital thermometer that quickly replaced the mercury bulb thermometer.

Since the development of the first electronic thermometer in 1969, IVAC has been a pioneer in the temperature taking market. In 1991, IVAC introduced the CORE•CHECK™ Tympanic Thermometer System, the latest milestone in the company's long history of innovation in clinical thermometry. This thermometer incorporates infrared technology to effectively measure temperatures with the highest level of clinical care and convenience.

"We are one of the top medical device firms in the nation—in research, manufacturing, and marketing of hospital-based drug infusion equipment," says William Hawkins, IVAC's president and CEO. "The future of our company lies in producing quality drug delivery systems, as well as a strong line of advanced vital signs measurement equipment."

The company's strategic research focus is on constantly improving the capability of its drug infusion systems. Utilizing sensor technology, IVAC's products provide save and effective delivery of medicines.

"Our focus on quality is what sets us apart from our competition," says Hawkins.

> "THE FUTURE OF OUR COMPANY LIES IN PRODUCING QUALITY DRUG DELIVERY SYSTEMS, AS WELL AS A STRONG LINE OF ADVANCED VITAL SIGNS MEASUREMENT EQUIPMENT," SAYS WILLIAM HAWKINS, IVAC'S PRESIDENT AND CEO.

GROWING SINCE 1986

More than two decades after its first product innovation, IVAC and its 1,200 employees produce several lines of sophisticated drug delivery systems and vital signs measurement products in a modern 370,000-square-foot building overlooking Sorrento Valley. Completed in 1980, the facility houses the company's corporate headquarters. Another plant, located in Creedmoor, North Carolina, manufactures the disposable accessories for IVAC's products. IVAC also has a disposable maquilladora assembly plant in Tijuana, Mexico.

IVAC was acquired in 1977 by Eli Lilly and Company, a world leader in the pharmaceuticals industry, and is now one of eight firms operated by Lilly's Medical Devices and Diagnostics Division. IVAC products are marketed and sold throughout the United States, Europe, the Pacific Rim, and Canada.

With these extensive resources in place, IVAC is well positioned to remain an important player in the medical technology field both in San Diego and across the globe.

Completed in 1980, IVAC's modern 370,000-square-foot building overlooking Sorrento Valley houses its corporate headquarters.

ABOVE: The IVAC SPACE•SAVER™ Pump and Model 570 Variable Pressure Pump.
LEFT: IVAC's CORE•CHECK™ Tympanic Thermometer System incorporates infrared technology to effectively measure temperatures with the highest level of clinical care and convenience.

A NEWLY PROPOSED CENTER CITY DEVELOPMENT CORPORATION PLAN, IF APPROVED BY THE CITY COUNCIL, WOULD STIMULATE MORE THAN $22 BILLION IN PRIVATE INVESTMENT DOWNTOWN OVER THE NEXT 35 YEARS.

1970-1992

1972

SHERATONS ON HARBOR ISLAND

1975

KOLODNY & PRESSMAN, A PROFESSIONAL CORPORATION

1976

LA JOLLA CANCER RESEARCH FOUNDATION

1983

GEN-PROBE INCORPORATED

1986

GENSIA PHARMACEUTICALS, INC.

1987

LIGAND PHARMACEUTICALS INCORPORATED

1988

OASIS SPORTS MEDICAL GROUP, INC.

1990

SAN DIEGO REGIONAL CANCER CENTER

SHERATONS ON HARBOR ISLAND

TT Sheraton Corporation has long been recognized for surpassing hospitality standards by providing its guests a first-class experience of service, accommodations, quality dining, and resort activities. And in Southern California, this industry giant has successfully mastered the balance of meeting business and leisure travelers' needs in the same location.

ITT Sheraton's thriving 1,050-room, two-hotel complex near downtown San Diego is just two minutes from San Diego's International Airport, which pleases the on-the-move business traveler. The waterfront hotels also have their own dock, marina, tennis courts, spa, swimming pools, health club, biking trails, and jogging paths: amenities which suit vacationers seeking relaxation.

A Major Role in San Diego
Built on an island in the harbor alongside the airport, the complex consists of two hotels: the Sheraton Harbor Island and the Sheraton Grand Harbor Island. Facing a colorful, boat-packed marina, the adjacent hotels are linked by tree-lined paths. The San Diego Harbor provides a constant parade of ships passing before a backdrop of the city's skyline.

Since their opening in the early 1970s, the hotels have played a major role in San Diego's cultural and business life, hosting functions for every facet of the city's population. Likewise, many major organizations have used the hotels as their convention headquarters.

The Sheratons on Harbor Island offer ocean-going whale watching trips from their own docks, while deep-sea fishing excursions are available nearby. The city's cruise ship terminal is also conveniently located. The much-used slogan "just minutes away" is always true when Sheraton refers to the San Diego Zoo, Sea Port Village, Old Town San Diego, Sea World, Old Globe Theater, and other local attractions. Maximum travel time is just 15 minutes, while Tijuana, Mexico is only 30 minutes away.

Superior Guest Amenities
The Sheraton Harbor Island Hotel, the larger of the two hotels, consists of 700 rooms, including a presidential suite and 24 VIP suites. It also boasts one of San Diego's outstanding restaurants, Merlano's, which is noted for its Italian cuisine. Catering to business travelers and conventions, the hotel seats up to 1,200 for dinner in its largest ballroom.

The Sheraton Grand Harbor Island, an upscale luxury hotel with 350 rooms, boasts 22 executive suites and two breathtaking penthouse suites. Its principal restaurant, Spencer's, is a popular San Diego

Situated on idyllic San Diego Bay, the Sheratons on Harbor Island offer a view of San Diego's skyline.

The Sheraton Harbor Island Hotel boasts one of San Diego's outstanding restaurants, Merlano's, which is noted for its Italian cuisine.

destination offering alfresco dining. Spencer's is also noted for its American-style cuisine, emphasizing seafood and steaks.

Physical fitness and recreation facilities are available in the complex, including four lighted tennis courts, a tennis pro shop, three heated swimming pools with a large sunning area and a poolside bar, a health club, men's and women's saunas, a whirlpool spa, and a five-mile jogging path. The health club, which has its own sport-clothing boutique, uses a full circuit of Nautilus equipment, alongside computerized stationary bikes, Lifesteps, and rowing machines. It also offers individual fitness evaluations and video aerobic exercise classes.

In 1990, the Sheratons on Harbor Island completed a multimillion dollar renovation in which all meeting space and guest rooms were refurbished. Since then, personal coffee service has been added to each room, and an executive lounge has been created for VIPs.

The hotels recently added voice mail as an in-room guest amenity, joining fewer than 2 percent of the nation's 70,000 hotels with this service.

A PART OF ITT SHERATON CORPORATION

The two hotels are operated by ITT Sheraton Corporation, the largest hotel network in the world, with nearly 450 hotels, inns, resorts, and all-suites operating in 62 countries. Each day, the company puts its long history of quality and service to work, hosting 25 million guests a year in its 126,882 hotel rooms worldwide.

Founded in Massachusetts in 1937, ITT Sheraton was the first U.S. hotelier to move into the interna-

tional marketplace, the first to be publicly traded on the New York Stock Exchange, the first to network hotel reservations with a telex system, the first to computerize its operations, and the first to offer a toll-free number for reservations.

ITT Sheraton's management has a reputation for innovation, tight controls, and strict operating guidelines, with intensive employee training particularly in guest service. General managers of individual properties are directed to achieve what ITT Sheraton's management consider their only product: a quality experience for every guest.

"It is personal service which will make customers choose ITT Sheraton and keep coming back," President and Chief Executive Officer John Kapioltas once told his employees. "Sheraton is a profit-oriented company, and the engine which drives those profits is personal, quality service. We believe service is the means to achieve the end goal of profits."

ITT Sheraton's thriving 1,050-room, two-hotel Harbor Island complex caters to vacationers and business travelers.

KOLODNY & PRESSMAN, A PROFESSIONAL CORPORATION

AN DIEGO, THE BIRTHPLACE OF CALIFORNIA, IS A city whose traditions are deeply embedded throughout the community. As an important center of trade, industry, and commerce for the Southwestern United States and the Pacific Rim, San Diego also offers great opportunity for growth, innovation, and change, attracting individuals and businesses who recognize the entrepreneurial, aggressive spirit alive in the city today.

One local organization that epitomizes contemporary San Diego is the highly visible law firm of Kolodny & Pressman. Its vitality, success, and competence clearly reflect the spirit of its attorneys and staff. In response to the changing needs of its growing clientele, Kolodny & Pressman has experienced steady, planned growth in keeping with its commitment to the needs of the community.

While always on the cutting edge of technological advances and innovation in the legal community, Kolodny & Pressman was founded in 1975 upon the traditional values of professionalism and excellence. Since then, the firm has demonstrated its commitment to strong relationships with clients and their needs. Although originally based in downtown San Diego, Kolodny & Pressman, in an attempt to be conveniently and centrally located, established new offices between the downtown San Diego/La Jolla areas and the fast-growing North San Diego County communities.

Kolodny & Pressman was founded in 1975 by Robert J. Kolodny and Joel M. Pressman.

"IT IS OUR RESPONSIBILITY AS ATTORNEYS TO BE MINDFUL OF OUR CLIENTS' GOALS AND DO WHATEVER IT TAKES TO OBTAIN THE BEST POSSIBLE RESULTS IN THE MOST PROFESSIONAL AND COST-EFFECTIVE MANNER," SAYS ROBERT J. KOLODNY.

THE BEST OF THE OLD AND THE NEW

The firm represents the best of the old and the new, drawing on conventional wisdom, adages, and rules for operating a law firm, while adopting innovative ideas necessary to take the firm into the 21st century.

The founding members of Kolodny & Pressman created a firm dedicated to developing and maintaining strong professional and personal attorney-client relationships. Today, the attorneys and staff at Kolodny & Pressman still strive to add a personal touch to all client affairs.

The firm's guiding philosophy is to aggressively and fairly represent clients, to practice law in a cost-effective manner, and to treat clients with fairness and respect in an atmosphere of professionalism and integrity. Kolodny & Pressman understands the importance of working with and treating clients as members of a team; of being accessible, responsive, honest, and forthright; of being involved with the community; of being accountable; of setting realistic goals; and of charging reasonable fees. As a result of this client-oriented philosophy, Kolodny & Pressman has become a major force in the San Diego legal community.

In response to pressure to increase the firm's size, the partners have resisted unmanaged growth, concentrating on the most pressing areas in today's legal environment. This focused flexibility allows the firm to expand and shift its resources to meet the changing needs of its clients. To that end, Kolodny & Pressman promotes specialization and encourages its members to concentrate on areas of substantive law that reflect the client's unique needs.

Robert J. Kolodny, one of the founding partners, summarizes the firm's philosophy: "We started with the commitment to do everything within our ability to achieve the best results for our clients. It is our responsibility as attorneys to be mindful of our clients' goals and do whatever it takes to obtain the best possible results in the most professional and cost-effective manner." According to senior litigation partner, Joel M. Pressman, "Our reputation is our most valued asset. People come to this firm out of choice. The obligation of our attorneys is to go the extra mile on behalf of all clients. This has been the key to our success."

The relative youth of Kolodny & Pressman's partners will allow the firm to vigorously continue its leadership role into the next century.

A MULTI-FACETED LAW FIRM

The firm offers service in a number of specialized areas that are generally divided among the transactional and trial departments. The transactional department includes a major real estate division, which represents clients in such matters as structuring complex real estate transactions and joint ventures. The section also represents clients in all phases of real estate development, including land use, entitlement, environmental, and common interest development matters.

The firm's real estate and loan workout practice group represents clients involved in transactions and workouts with financial institutions and various governmental agencies. The group also has extensive experience in working with the Resolution Trust Corporation (RTC). The firm represents clients interested in realizing opportunities from distressed real estate held by the RTC and other government agencies through negotiation of loan workouts, acquisitions, or contracting with government agencies, financial institutions, and the RTC.

The firm has additional departments which handle all aspects of business law, including the formation of new business entities and the representation of an impressive and growing group of local and international businesses; tax planning; planning and implementing the business needs of health care professionals; estate planning and administration of decedents' estates, including risk analysis, probate, formation,

and trust administration; administrative law; and high technology and intellectual property matters.

The litigation department handles many kinds of litigation, including complex real estate matters (construction defects, land use, development, and mechanic's liens), diverse tort matters, and complex business litigation issues (entity disputes, fraud, securities, and banking). The litigation department has grown and gained notoriety in recent years due, in large part, to its many successes in the courtroom and its large business-oriented jury verdicts. The appellate section of the litigation department has also won landmark decisions.

The trial department litigates cases in state, federal, and bankruptcy courts and works closely with the risk analysis section of the transactional department. This cooperation helps clients to identify and recognize potential risks in existing and prospective ventures and to plan alternative ways to structure future transactions.

Law firms of the future will learn from, emulate, and reflect on today's experiences and innovative concepts. The relative youth of Kolodny & Pressman's partners will allow the firm to vigorously continue its leadership role into the next century. As a firm of talented professionals who are committed to the community, dedicated to excellence, and concerned for their clients' well-being, Kolodny & Pressman is prepared to remain an excellent model for the legal profession far into the future.

GEN-PROBE INCORPORATED

P ROBING THE GENES OF MANKIND — THE VERY building blocks of life—has propelled a local company to a position of leadership in the nation's biotechnology industry. Gen-Probe, founded in San Diego in 1983, is a U.S. leader in developing and marketing medical products based on genetic probe technology. Allowing faster speed and accuracy in diagnosing human disease, genetic probing is destined to change the way medicine is practiced.

"We introduced the world's first instrument-reagent system to perform direct genetic probe diagnosis of specimens in a non-radioactive format," says President and Chief Executive Officer Thomas A. Bologna. "With our technology, we have a complete testing system for organisms causing two sexually-transmitted diseases, *Chlamydia trachomatis* and *Neisseria gonorrhoeae*."

GEN-PROBE WAS ONE OF THE FIRST COMPANIES TO MAKE THE TRANSITION FROM RESEARCH AND DEVELOPMENT TO A FULLY-INTEGRATED ENTERPRISE THAT RESEARCHES, MANUFACTURES, AND MARKETS MEDICAL PRODUCTS USING GENETIC PROBE TECHNOLOGY.

Experts long ago predicted that genetic probes would likely be the technology of choice for future diagnosticians. That future is here. Gen-Probe has accelerated research programs aimed at improving the diagnosis of not only bacterial infections such as *Chlamydia* and *Neisseria gonorrhoeae*, but also viral infections and cancer.

MEETING THE NEEDS OF THE MARKETPLACE
Today, Gen-Probe is a wholly-owned subsidiary of Chugai Pharmaceutical Co., Ltd. of Tokyo and operates under almost complete autonomy. Gen-Probe's 68,000-square-foot plant at 9880 Campus Point Drive contains administrative offices, labs, and manufacturing lines. Two other facilities, totaling 21,000 square feet, on Rehco Road in San Diego house additional manufacturing and warehousing space.

"We are big on research and development," says Bologna. "We have a large group of individuals working on genetic probe-based technologies. We are changing the way medicine is practiced through our technology. Our focus is on research and development that meets the needs of the marketplace as it relates to our technology."

"We make unconventional products, innovative products; no 'me, too' products," says President and CEO Thomas A. Bologna. "Our reward is increased sales of products that benefit mankind."

FROM AN R&D ENTITY TO A FULLY INTEGRATED ENTERPRISE
Hospitals and reference labs use the unique quick-diagnosis assay reagents and associated instruments pioneered by Gen-Probe. With Gen-Probe assays, patients are able to undergo appropriate therapy earlier, resulting in shorter hospital stays, reduction in the spread of infectious diseases, and a general evolution in medical diagnostics. In fact, Gen-Probe was one of the first companies to make the transition from research and development to a fully-integrated enterprise that researches, manufactures, and markets medical products using genetic probe technology.

"The company's core technology stands as the key stroke that started the company going," says Bologna. "It propelled genetic probes from the confines of the research setting into the first commercial test kits for clinical lab use. Known as the in-solution targeting of ribosomal RNA, it is up to 10,000 times more sensitive than competitive techniques which directly target non-amplified DNA."

Clean, high quality conditions are maintained from product concept through shipment to the customer.

Gen-Probe's future is promising. "We make unconventional, innovative products; no 'me, too' products," says Bologna. "The technology is powerful, and it has proven to be of real value to both the physician and the patient. Product sales are our major thrust today. We now have over 25 products on the market. And our reward is increased sales of products that benefit mankind."

The company's major product line includes systems based on instruments known as the LEADER™ and reagents known as PACE™ that provide quick, direct detection of *Chlamydia* and *N. gonorrhoeae*. The company's AccuProbe product line includes reagents for rapid detection of over 18 organisms from culture media and is used with a smaller Gen-Probe instrument.

Institute, the medical school at the University of California at San Diego, Scripps Clinic and Research Foundation, and a host of entrepreneurial companies, all of which have given the city a reputation as a new center for biotechnology.

This grouping of scientists, educators, and researchers has led to the development of a supportive business climate, as well as associated companies such as specialized law firms, venture capital experts, and a large work force of highly trained technicians.

"That's precisely why we are here and why we plan to stay," says Bologna. "San Diego has a strong, supportive infrastructure, and academic and scientific professionals have good interaction with the business community. Gen-Probe is a part of that interaction and proud of it. We are committed to San Diego."

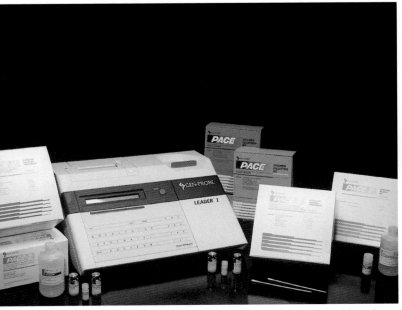

Gen-Probe's major product line, comprised of the LEADER™ and PACE™, is the world's first genetic probe instrument/reagent system to provide quick, direct detection of Chlamydia and N. gonorrhoeae.

"Traditionally, lab diagnostics have been done by growing cultures; this could take from several days to weeks or even months," says Bologna. "We do the analysis directly from the specimen, break down the cell, hybridize the nucleic acid, and detect the causative agent in a matter of hours."

Much of Gen-Probe's technology is proprietary, developed in its own labs, but it also uses other complementary technologies for which it has rights. Bologna equates the procedure to an aircraft or automobile maker combining various technologies to make an end product.

PART OF A SUPPORTIVE BUSINESS CLIMATE
Gen-Probe fits right into San Diego's large colony of medically-related biotech companies. Spawned by San Diego's reputation as a research center, the firms were attracted by the potential for synergy with Salk

ABOVE: Gen-Probe's corporate headquarters is located on Campus Point Drive in San Diego.
LEFT: Automated boxing equipment used for assembly of PACE 2 Specimen Collection Kits helps streamline the manufacturing process at Gen-Probe.

GENSIA PARMACEUTICALS, INC.

AN DIEGO HAS LONG BEEN RECOGNIZED AS A MAJOR biotech center. Over the last two decades, about 100 biotech companies have emerged locally, discovering many medical diagnostic products and developing new methods of treating disease. A standout in that industry is Gensia Pharmaceuticals, Inc., a relatively young but well-respected firm that is developing new drugs that can be used to treat and diagnose cardiovascular disease and treat stroke and neurological diseases such as epilepsy.

"The potential for the industry is tremendous," says David F. Hale, Gensia's chairman, president, and chief executive officer. "Collectively, we are on the verge of discovering the basis for many diseases, and much of the significant research is being done in biotechnology. There is the very real potential to improve the quality of people's lives."

A CLIMATE OF INNOVATION

The local biotech industry blossomed in the late 1970s and early 1980s, based on the ground-breaking work being done at the local research triumvirate: the University of California at San Diego (UCSD), the Salk Institute, and the Scripps Clinic and Research Foundation. Since its emergence, the biotech industry has required large amounts of risk capital to underwrite the years of scientific research and development, preclinical and human clinical testing, the rigors and time required to obtain government approvals, and the high cost of subsequent marketing.

Amid this climate of innovation, Gensia was founded in 1986 to focus on the discovery, development, manufacturing, and marketing of pioneer pharmaceutical products for the acute care hospital market. Located north of San Diego in Sorrento Valley, Gensia is today one of the city's largest biopharmaceutical companies and employs approximately 275 people in San Diego and Irvine, California and the United Kingdom. Gensia has been able to

"OUR GOAL IS TO DEVELOP GENSIA INTO A RESEARCH-BASED BIOPHARMACEUTICAL COMPANY THAT DISCOVERS, DEVELOPS, MANUFACTURES, AND MARKETS DRUGS ON A WORLDWIDE BASIS," SAYS DAVID F. HALE, GENSIA'S CHAIRMAN, PRESIDENT, AND CHIEF EXECUTIVE OFFICER.

steadily move its research toward commercialization by achieving specific, established goals on time.

Gensia is a public company traded on the NASDAQ exchange ticker symbol: (GNSA). Four public stock offerings, including the formation of a new public company called Aramed, Inc. (ARAMZ), and a research and development limited partnership have been successful, providing evidence of investors' confidence in the firm's management and its potential to produce long-term rewards.

In addition, Gensia has a major strategic alliance with Marion Merrell Dow, Inc. to develop and sell orally active versions (capsule or tablet products) of its adenosine regulating agent (ARA) drugs for the treatment of cardiovascular and cerebrovascular diseases. Serendipity led to a discovery by Gensia scientists relating to the regulation of glucose production. As a result of this breakthrough, Gensia entered into a research and development agreement with Sandoz Pharmaceutical Corporation in January 1992 to discover and develop drugs for the treatment of Type II diabetes. Through an Irvine, California subsidiary—Gensia Laboratories, Ltd.—Gensia manufactures and sells a line of multi-source injectable pharmaceuticals for the acute care hospital market. The company also has a subsidiary, Gensia Europe, Ltd., in the United Kingdom.

FOCUSING ON RESEARCH

The company's primary research focus is in the area of purine and pyrimidine metabolism. Purines and pyrimidines, essential molecules in the body, are the building blocks of genetic materials such as DNA and RNA. They also play an important role as co-factors and regulators of important biological functions.

Arasine™, Gensia's first ARA drug currently in the final stage of clinical testing, is being developed for use in patients undergoing coronary artery bypass surgery to minimize heart attacks and other adverse cardiovascular events associated with the surgery.

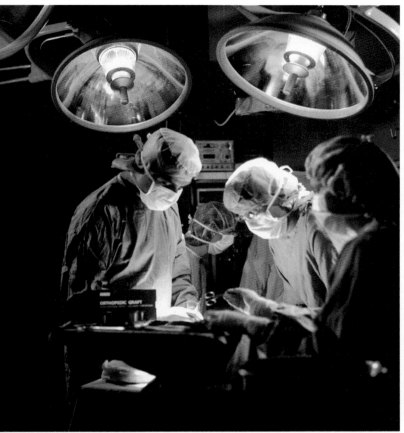

Arasine™, one of Gensia's cardiovascular drugs, may be effective in reducing adverse cardiovascular events associated with coronary artery bypass graft surgery.

Arasine and second generation ARAs will also be evaluated for use as cardioprotective agents in non-cardiac surgery, acute myocardial infarction (heart attack), unstable angina, and coronary angioplasty. In addition, orally active drugs that Gensia is developing with Marion Merrell Dow will be evaluated for use in the treatment of chronic cardiovascular diseases.

Final clinical testing is beginning on arbutamine, the Gensia drug which is combined with a computer-controlled drug delivery device, together called the GenESA™ System. It is used to pharmacologically simulate the cardiovascular effects of exercise to diagnose heart problems in patients unable to undergo or endure traditional exercise-stress testing on a treadmill. The GenESA System has been described as a more versatile and convenient alternative for testing certain patients who are known or suspected to have coronary artery disease. Other drugs in various stages of research and development include ARA compounds focused on the treatment of stroke, epilepsy, and other seizure disorders and glucose-lowering purine compounds for the treatment of Type II diabetes.

MORE THAN A GOOD IDEA
The idea for Gensia was conceived by two UCSD scientists—Harry E. Gruber, M.D. and Paul K.

Laikind, Ph.D.—as a means of developing therapeutic products based on Dr. Gruber's early work with ARA technology. Today, Gruber is vice president for research, while Laikind serves as vice president for ARA development and technology licensing.

David Hale, a veteran of the pharmaceutical business, was previously employed by Becton Dickinson & Company and Ortho Pharmaceuticals, a division of Johnson & Johnson. Recruited to San Diego in 1982 as senior vice president of marketing and business development for Hybritech Incorporated (a pioneer in monoclonal antibodies), Hale became president of the firm in 1983. In 1986, Hybritech was acquired by Eli Lilly and Company. Hale joined Gensia in June 1987 as president and chief executive officer with little more than a scientific theory, an empty building, two scientists, one lab technician, and a receptionist. Today, he is widely regarded as the biotech industry's San Diego spokesman—a talented entrepreneur with an impressive track record and a promising future.

"Strategically, our goal is to make Gensia into a fully integrated biopharmaceutical company, manufacturing and marketing drugs on a worldwide basis," says Hale, who became Gensia's chairman of the board in 1991. "We have the strategy, the scientists, and the management capability to do it."

Gensia's scientists are working to develop new drugs for the treatment of cardiovascular disease, stroke, epilepsy, and diabetes.

Historically, discoveries of new medical drugs have depended on basic scientific research and a lot of human intuition. San Diego's Ligand Pharmaceuticals Incorporated is attempting to speed up the process with its own brand of technology—a unique combination of laboratory experiments and a base of biological discoveries originating at the Salk Institute.

The Ligand-Salk partnership is often cited as evidence of the synergy between San Diego's proprietary biotech industry and its biological research institutes, forming a mutually beneficial association that has drawn international recognition to the area.

FOCUSED ON INTRACELLULAR TECHNOLOGY

Five-year-old Ligand Pharmaceuticals is striving to develop totally new drug systems based on intracellular receptor technology. The company's scientists are seeking drugs similar to natural hormones that interact with intracellular receptors. Such activity is called a ligand interaction, the process from which the company took its name. Drugs that create a ligand interaction have great potential for treating a variety of diseases, including arthritis, heart disease, osteoporosis, and several forms of cancer.

"We are the only company in the United States focused on intracellular technology," says Howard C. Birndorf, chairman emeritus and former president and chief executive officer.

Widely known as an entrepreneur and a leader in San Diego's biotech industry, Birndorf is a unique example of a scientist-turned-businessman. The co-founder of three major San Diego biotech firms—Hybritech, Gen-Probe, and Idec—he also assisted in establishing Gensia Pharmaceuticals. Likewise, Birndorf has served on the boards of Gen-Probe, Idec, Gensia, and the University of California at San Diego Cancer Center.

Birndorf, who holds a graduate degree in biochemistry, joined Ligand after successful stints as a vice president of Hybritech, the nation's largest monoclonal antibody-based firm (sold to Eli Lilly in 1986), and Gen-Probe, the most successful exploiter of nucleic acid hybridization technology (purchased by Chugai Pharmaceutical Co. of Japan in 1988). Known for his skills in raising venture capital, attracting top scientists, and acquiring sophisticated research technology, Birndorf also brings the management experience and a sense of urgency that biotech start-ups need to survive during the critical first years.

Ligand was co-founded by Birndorf in 1988, along with Ronald M. Evans, Ph.D., a Salk Institute scientist who made the important base discoveries in intracellular hormone receptors. In 1989, Ligand moved into its new 21,000-square-foot facility in La Jolla's Golden Triangle area, the heart of one of America's premier biotech development centers near such prestigious medical research institutions as Salk,

Ligand's management team of Chairman Emeritus Howard Birndorf and President and CEO David Robinson combines entrepreneurship and experienced pharmaceutical leadership.

Ligand occupies 22,000 square feet of office and research space in La Jolla's Golden Triangle.

the Scripps Clinic and Research Foundation, and the
University of California at San Diego.

SOPHISTICATED RESEARCH STAFF AND EQUIPMENT

The company's six research departments employ 65
scientists and a variety of support staff. According to
company policy, Ligand combines experienced and
highly specialized professionals from diagnostic, research, and pharmaceutical institutes and companies
into groups, creating interdisciplinary teams. All
senior research personnel hold doctoral degrees and
have industrial and clinical experience. Most have
held postdoctoral positions at other research centers.

Ligand's state-of-the-art laboratories are equipped
to perform research in biochemistry, drug screening,
cell biology, pharmacology, molecular biology, medici-
nal chemistry, and computerized research. In addition, the company's compound screening assay system
has been automated with robotic work stations in
order to do high-volume screening. Its computer
network ensures a flow of research data from scientific
instruments to a central data processing system.
Ligand's computers track a massive compound inven-
tory, perform statistical analysis, and provide the
capacity for DNA sequence analysis.

"We have come a long way in a short time," says
Birndorf. "We are on the cutting edge of biological
research, with many discoveries ahead of us. Our
current assets are our people and our technology."

Many scientists believe that intracellular receptor
technology will lead to the discovery of drugs to treat
diseases for which there are currently no viable
treatment alternatives. Research of the kind being
done at Ligand may also help create drugs to replace
less effective ones. Though worldwide sales for the
biotech industry are expected to one day exceed $30
billion annually, the accompanying benefits to mankind are incalculable. There is also a potential for the
discovery of new receptors that could yield medicines
to mediate cholesterol and detoxify, lead to specific
new approaches to infectious diseases that are difficult
to treat with available drugs, and establish new classes
of insecticides and herbicides.

"Our goal is to discover and develop more
efficacious drugs that will ultimately benefit mankind," explains Birndorf. "Our strategy is to accom-
plish the research, the clinical and human trials, and
the development that will allow us to become a fully
integrated pharmaceutical company."

Evidence of Birndorf's commitment to that goal is
his recent recruitment of David E. Robinson, former
chief operating officer of the Italian pharmaceutical
giant, Erbamont. As the company's new president and
chief executive officer, Robinson may be the most
senior pharmaceutical executive ever recruited to lead
a start-up company. However, Birndorf believes that
Ligand's technology is so broad-based that strategic
direction should be committed to a seasoned executive from the pharmaceutical industry.

OASIS SPORTS MEDICAL GROUP, INC.

N ONE ROOM, A FOOTBALL PLAYER FOR THE SAN Diego Chargers undergoes push-pull therapy for an injured thigh. In another, an attorney is treated for a muscle pulled while jogging.

Down a corridor, two surgeons discuss the merits of surgery versus medication and therapy as they examine a sophisticated magnetic resonance image of the knee of a San Diego Sockers player.

In yet another room, a bricklayer learns the news that high tech arthroscopic knee surgery will have him back at work in a few weeks.

Meanwhile, a classroom of football players, weekend athletes, and desk jockies with back problems hear a lecture on how to prevent injuries. And elsewhere, an athletic trainer and an exercise physiologist modify a knee brace to fit a swimmer in training for the Olympics.

AT OASIS, ADVANCED, OFTEN PIONEERING, SPORTS MEDICINE TECHNIQUES SOLVE PROBLEMS FOR BIG-TIME ATHLETES, AS WELL AS EVERYDAY SPORTS ENTHUSIASTS.

Welcome to the OASIS Sports Medical Group, where advanced, often pioneering, sports medicine techniques solve problems for big-time athletes, as well as everyday sports enthusiasts.

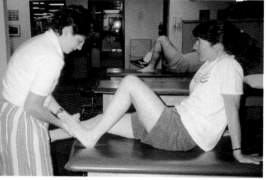

An OASIS physical therapist instructs a patient in rehabilitation techniques after surgery.

ORTHOPAEDIC, ARTHROSCOPIC & SPORTS INJURY SPECIALISTS

OASIS is an acronym for the goals and duties of the facility's 55 doctors, surgeons, therapists, technicians, and administrators. The letters stand for Orthopaedic, Arthroscopic & Sports Injury Specialists, but thousands of San Diegans have discovered that it is indeed an oasis where return to normal living is the objective.

"The demands of age, the level of competition, the type of sport, and the occupations of our patients vary widely," explains Dr. Gary Losse. "We try to understand our patients' goals. Then we help them overcome the injury hurdle so they can get back to work—whether it is on the football field or in the courtroom, driving a truck or performing at the ballet."

Losse organized OASIS in 1988 as a logical outgrowth of associations he and other surgeons have had with major sports teams. The practice is built around insuring long-term health; offering primary day-to-day medical care, such as pre-season physicals and injury prevention; and providing treatment, surgery, and follow-up therapy.

Previously a physician for the San Francisco 49ers and San Diego State Aztecs, Dr. Losse has been chief physician for the San Diego Chargers football team for 12 years. He also serves as the doctor in charge of both the San Diego Gulls hockey team and the America3 sailors.

But he is certainly not alone at OASIS in his experience with professional athletes and general sports medicine. In addition to duties with the San Diego Chargers and Sockers, Dr. Daniel B. Robertson, a diplomate of the American Board of Orthopaedic Surgeons, specializes in total hip and knee replacements.

Dr. Richard S. Gilbert, team podiatrist for the Chargers and Gulls, serves as a consultant to the U.S. Men's and Women's Volleyball team. Also at OASIS are Dr. Kent Feldman, a podiatrist, and Dr. Jerry Hizon, a board-certified family practitioner and assistant clinical professor at the University of California in Irvine.

SPREADING THE WORD ON SPORTS MEDICINE TECHNOLOGY

Beyond their duties in the offices, examining rooms, and laboratories of the OASIS facility, all staff members lecture on sports medicine throughout the United States and abroad, relating the advanced techniques developed at OASIS.

The staff also holds free classes for sports managers on such topics as sideline injury management, decision-making on return to participation, legal liability, and taping and bracing. And they answer general questions from the public on a 24-hour sports injury hotline (800) 800-OASIS, fulfilling an important community involvement goal of the medical group.

According to the *San Diego Tribune,* Losse's "willingness to go the extra step and his innovations in arthroscopy place him at the forefront among orthopedists in this country."

Undoubtedly, each member of the OASIS staff strives to maintain this same level of innovation and medical expertise for every patient—from the professional athlete to the weekend jogger.

Dr. Gary Losse treats the injury of a San Diego Chargers player during a game.

SAN DIEGO REGIONAL CANCER CENTER

HE SAN DIEGO REGIONAL CANCER CENTER IS THE newest member of a community of researchers that has contributed to San Diego's national status as a biotechnology center. The Regional Cancer Center stands out because of its unique research and its location in La Jolla's Torrey Pines Mesa, where the synergism of educators, researchers, hospitals, and biotech firms almost daily creates new possibilities for miracle drugs and potential cures.

In 1990, Dr. Ivor Royston, a renowned cancer researcher at the University of California San Diego, organized a group of community physicians committed to basic research and to delivering the benefits of that research to patients quickly. Today, the Cancer Center is the only institution in the United States researching cancer with a focus on immunotherapy and gene therapy. It also practices an innovative combination of research with clinical trials on patients.

> **"WE TRY OUT THE NOVEL TECHNIQUES AS SOON AS POSSIBLE," SAYS DR. IVOR ROYSTON, PRESIDENT AND SCIENTIFIC DIRECTOR. "OUR MISSION IS TO BRIDGE THE LABORATORY AND THE BEDSIDE—TO TAKE GROUNDBREAKING LAB DISCOVERIES AND SPEED THEM TO THE PATIENT."**

"Unprecedented lab discoveries involving the human immune system and the genetics of cancer are leading to new treatment approaches," says Royston, president and scientific director of the center. "By focusing on the origins of cancer, these discoveries hold the promise of real cures."

A MAJOR RESEARCH FACILITY

The center maintains affiliations with local hospitals and cancer specialists to deliver sophisticated, cutting-edge research to patients. In addition, it has strategic plans to open its own outpatient clinic, ultimately becoming a major research and cancer care facility, as well as a regional resource for cancer researchers and oncologists far into the 21st century.

Royston is a recognized authority in cancer research, particularly in the development of monoclonal antibodies which can be used diagnostically and therapeutically in cancer management. He served as director of clinical immunology at the UCSD Cancer Center before organizing the San Diego Regional Cancer Center. Royston, who remains an adjunct professor of medicine at UCSD, was a founder of San Diego-based Hybritech, a leading biotechnology company that has since been sold to Eli Lilly & Co. Royston also co-founded IDEC Pharmaceuticals Corp. and GeneSys Therapeutics Corp.

Located in the La Jolla Spectrum Science Park, the Cancer Center employs 40 people, with a ratio of three scientist-researchers for every member of its support staff. The nonprofit institution began with an $800,000 federal cancer research grant and is currently funded by other grants and private contributions.

The center's board of trustees consists of community, business, and medical leaders. Its chairman is Thomas Shiftan, M.D., an oncologist, who is chief of the Department of Medicine at Sharp Memorial Hospital. Other board members include Royston; Robert Barone, M.D. and Allan Goodman, M.D., both surgeons; and Dennis J. Carlo, Ph.D., Sidney Green, Christine Forester, Mitchell Ellner, and Stephen Kandel.

"Laboratory research discoveries do not aid patients unless coupled with clinical research which leads to effective treatment," says Royston. "We try out the novel techniques as soon as possible. Our mission is to bridge the laboratory and the bedside—to take groundbreaking lab discoveries and speed them to the patient."

LEFT: In 1990, Dr. Ivor Royston organized a group of community physicians committed to basic research and to delivering the benefits of that research to patients quickly.

LA JOLLA CANCER RESEARCH FOUNDATION

CCASIONALLY, THE NATION'S PREMIER BIOLOGISTS refer to La Jolla as "Boston West," or discuss a "Boston-La Jolla academic-research axis." Their conversations usually revolve around the significant discoveries made by the cluster of biological research institutes in La Jolla compared to their East Coast academic counterparts.

The La Jolla Cancer Research Foundation has always stood out as a member of this unrelated band of local institutions—with such names as Salk, Scripps, and University of California at San Diego—upon which an entire entrepreneurial biotech industry has relied for nearly two decades. The La Jolla Cancer Research Foundation's uniqueness in this community of excellence is based upon its contributions to scientific knowledge, as measured by both the quality of its research and its consequent standing in national and international medical circles.

THE FOUNDATION STANDS OUT AMONG SIMILAR FACILITIES BECAUSE OF ITS UNIQUE BLENDING OF CANCER RESEARCH AND DEVELOPMENTAL BIOLOGY. "TO UNCOVER MOLECULAR KEYS TO ABNORMAL CELL BEHAVIOR THAT LEADS TO CANCER, WE NEED BASIC RESEARCH," SAYS DR. ERKKI RUOSLAHTI, PRESIDENT AND CHIEF EXECUTIVE OFFICER.

SIGNIFICANT DISCOVERIES IN CANCER RESEARCH

Though 16 years old, the nonprofit, independent La Jolla Cancer Research Foundation is a relative newcomer in the quest for a cancer cure. Its unique, focused approach, however, has already led to a series of significant discoveries in cell adhesion, cell surface carbohydrates, and tumor markers. Along the way, researchers have made ancillary discoveries in the fields of kidney disease and wound healing.

Some of the nation's most basic cancer cell research is being done in the Foundation's labs, charting new territory for exploration by the scientific community. Since 1981, the institute has been one of only 15 laboratories in the nation designated as a basic research facility by the National Cancer Institute, the federal organization which oversees cancer research.

Dr. Erkki Ruoslahti, the Foundation's president and chief executive officer, has pioneered research in how cancer cells and normal cells adhere to other cells and to a mesh work known as the extracellular matrix. Widely acclaimed as a cell biologist, Ruoslahti devotes his time to the laboratory and to overseeing the institute.

Indeed, the Foundation stands out among similar facilities because of its unique blending of cancer research and developmental biology. "To uncover molecular keys to abnormal cell behavior that leads to cancer, we need basic research," says Ruoslahti.

GROWTH SINCE 1976

The Foundation was started in 1976 with an annual grant budget of $150,000. The first lab was in a rented space in downtown La Jolla. In 1978, the Foundation received a gift of five acres of land on North Torrey Pines Road.

From such modest beginnings, the Foundation has grown to a complex of three laboratory buildings and a library on a nine-acre campus. Another 35,000-square-foot laboratory building is slated to be built. There are currently 24 major research projects under way, each headed by a principal investigator. With an annual budget of $15 million, the Foundation employs 250 people, including 100 individuals that hold doctoral level degrees.

In 1987, Foundation technology contributed to the inception of Telios Pharmaceuticals, Inc., a company that develops drugs and therapeutic agents based on Foundation discoveries.

Another distinguishing characteristic of the Foundation—and probably the one most responsible for its rapid rise as a research leader—is a unique scientific work environment that lacks the frustrations of bureaucracy. "We have always put the scientists' research projects ahead of everything else," says Ruoslahti. "That's very important. When combined with our distinct goals, our entrepreneurial philosophy enables us to gain new insight into cancer."

RIGHT: Some of the nation's most basic cancer cell research is being done at the La Jolla Cancer Research Foundation, charting new territory for exploration by the scientific community.

PHOTOGRAPHERS

PHOTO EDITOR JERRY RIFE, a native San Diegan, has been a staff photographer for the *San Diego Union-Tribune* since 1963. A graduate of San Diego State University, Rife has won over 60 annual photography awards from the National Press Photographers Association, California Press Photographers Association, California Newspaper Publishers Association, Society of Newspaper Design, Society of Professional Journalists, San Diego Press Club, Copley Newspapers, Associated Press, Freedoms Foundation, and numerous international juried art exhibitions.

He is the author of over 150 newspaper and magazine articles on photographic criticism, photographic history, and the use of photography in the news media.

He and his wife, Jan, are co-authors of numerous travel articles on Mexico, Spain, and Portugal. His other foreign assignments have included Columbia, Chile, Peru, and the Philippines.

JAMES BAIRD, originally from Glen Cove, New York, received his B.A. in communications from the University of Illinois in 1973. A photographer for the *San Diego Union-Tribune* since 1985, Baird has also worked for the *Escondido Times-Advocate* and St. Louis' *Metro-East Journal.*

CHRIS CAVANAUGH specializes in photojournalism with a special emphasis in documentary photography. A native of San Diego, Cavanaugh worked for the *San Diego Union-Tribune* from 1986-92. In 1991 she established a Southern California chapter of the women's committee of the National Press Photographers Association.

NELVIN CEPEDA, a native of Guam, has worked as a photographer for the *San Diego Union-Tribune* and for the U.S. Army. In recent years he has won awards at the International Exposition of Photography at Del Mar, California, at a photography contest sponsored by the U.S. military, and from the San Diego Photojournalism Society.

BARRY FITZSIMMONS has been a photograher for the *San Diego Union-Tribune* 19 years; since 1987 he has also served as photo lab supervisor. He attended San Diego State University and has taught photography at Miramar Community College. Published worldwide in magazines, newspapers, and books, Fitzsimmons has also won many national and international awards.

MICHAEL PAUL FRANKLIN, a staff photographer for the *San Diego Union-Tribune*, has worked on special projects in Mexico and California's Central Valley documenting the lives of agricultural workers. Franklin has received awards from the National Press Photographers Association and the National Conference of Christians and Jews.

ROBERT GAUTHIER has been employed by the *San Diego Union-Tribune* for four years. A 1983 graduate of Fresno State University, Gauthier has also worked as a photographer for the *Escondido Times-Advocate* and the *Rancho Bernardo News.* He and his wife and two children live in Escondido, California.

JOHN GIBBINS, a third-generation San Diegan, graduated from San Diego State University with a B.A. in journalism. A staff photographer for the *San Diego Union-Tribune*, Gibbins also does free-lance work for Reuters News Pictures. He has a special interest in covering Latin American issues.

DON KOHLBAUER, a photographer for the *San Diego Union-Tribune*, graduated from the U.S. Naval School of Photography in 1974. Some of his special assignments at the *Tribune* have included the 1988 Republican Convention in New Orleans and the 1984 National Baseball League play-offs and World Series.

MARTI KRANZBERG is a free-lance photojournalist. She graduated in 1976 from Webster University in St. Louis, Missouri, her hometown, and in 1979 moved to San Diego. Her photos have been published in numerous area publications. From 1986-90 she produced videos for a visitor information network.

TOM KURTZ is a free-lance photographer based in San Diego. As a photographer for the *San Diego Union-Tribune* from 1985-92, he specialized in editorial photography. He particularly enjoys working on either side of the U.S./Mexico border on issues such as migration and cross-culturalism.

HOWARD LIPIN joined the *San Diego Union-Tribune* as a staff photographer in 1986 after having worked at three smaller newspapers in California. His work has appeared in national magazines and books, and he has won numerous local, regional, and national photography awards. Lipin and his wife are expecting their second child in July 1992.

J. T. MacMillan earned his bachelor's degree in journalism in 1984 from the University of Arizona. He worked as a staff photographer for the *San Diego Union-Tribune* from 1989-92. Through his work on travel articles, he is developing an expertise in underwater photography.

Abigail Kurtz Mahoney is a free-lance photographic retoucher who also does commercial, portrait, and fine art photography. A native of Michigan, Mahoney has exhibited widely and won numerous awards in California photography competitions.

Rick McCarthy, deceased, was a staff photographer for the *San Diego Union-Tribune* from 1970-88. McCarthy won several awards from national and international organizations including the Associated Press News Executive Council and the World Press Photo Holland Foundation. He served as a field photographer for the Navy from 1965-1969 during the Vietnam War.

Gerald McClard, a professional photographer for 15 years, is a staff photographer for the *San Diego Union-Tribune*. He has covered national and international events including the 1984 Olympics in Los Angeles, the tour of the United States by Pope John Paul II in 1987, and the plight of Amerasian children in Vietnam.

John R. McCutchen has worked at the *San Diego Union-Tribune* for four years. Raised in East Peoria, Illinois, he was a photographer at the *Southern Illinoisan* in Carbondale from 1980-88. A winner of many state and regional photography awards, McCutchen covered the war in the Persian Gulf from Saudia Arabia, Kuwait, and Iraq.

John Nelson joined the *San Diego Union-Tribune* as a staff photographer in 1989. Before that he worked for the *Escondido Times-Advocate* from 1986-89. Nelson graduated from California State University at Fresno in 1985 with a B.A. in journalism. He has a special interest in portrait photography.

Charlie Neuman covers the north county as a photographer for the *San Diego Union-Tribune*. A graduate of Oceanside High School in north San Diego County, Neuman has over the last 12 years worked for three daily newspapers in San Diego County. Neuman considers newspaper work—especially feature photography—his favorite kind of photography.

Louise A. Palazola is a self-employed photographer who specializes in fine art portraiture and photo illustration and exhibits her work widely. A graduate of the University of Denver, Palazola has taken advanced courses at the Winchester School of Art in England and at the Brooks Institute of Photography in Santa Barbara, California.

Jennie Redfield, a native Southern Californian, is a professional free-lance photographer who specializes in commercial and portrait photography. Her work has been exhibited and published locally, and she has won recognition at the International Exposition of Photography at Del Mar, California.

Bill Romero is a free-lance photojournalist with 18 years' experience. From 1979-92 he worked at the *San Diego Union-Tribune*. For the newspaper he covered the 1984 Summer Olympics in Los Angeles, and in 1986 he won the second place award in color features in the Baseball Hall of Fame photography contest.

Dave Siccardi operates his own studio in San Diego specializing in editorial and commercial food photography. Originally from Denver, Colorado, Siccardi is a former photographer for the *San Diego Union-Tribune*. His most memorable news assignment at the *Tribune* was the 1988 Democratic National Convention in Atlanta.

James Skovmand has been a news photographer in San Diego County for 14 years and a staffer for the *San Diego Union-Tribune* for the last 10. He won eight local and national awards in 1990 for his work documenting relief efforts in Romania.

Charley Starr, a native of Chula Vista, California, has been a professional photographer for more than 10 years, most of that time at the *San Diego Union-Tribune*. He has also worked for the *Orange Coast Daily Pilot* and the *Anaheim Bulletin*. A sailboat enthusiast himself, Starr will cover the America's Cup race in San Diego in May 1992.

Jack Yon is a free-lance advertising photographer who lives in Santee, California. While a staff photographer at the *San Diego Union-Tribune* from 1988-92, he pursued a special interest in portrait and fashion photography. Yon won the top award for sports photography from the San Diego Press Club in 1989, and in 1990 won an award for the best sports photograph in a competition among all California daily newspapers.

I N THE WORLD'S EYES, SAN DIEGO IS THE NEW BELLE OF
THE BALL WITH SUITORS LINING UP FOR A SPACE ON HER
DANCE CARD.

INDEX TO PATRONS

JERRY RIFE

SAN DIEGO'S CLIMATE, LOCATION, AND WONDERFUL NATURAL HARBOR HAVE ALWAYS HELD A GOLDEN PROMISE FOR WESTERN PIONEERS. NOW THAT PROMISE IS REACHING FULFILLMENT AS SAN DIEGO EMERGES AS AN INTERNATIONAL PRESENCE.